THE
SCIENCE
ALMANAC
FOR
KIDS

By Q. L. Pearce
Illustrated by Mary Bryson
and Mary Ann Fraser

LOWELL HOUSE JUVENILE

LOS ANGELES

NTC/Contemporary Publishing Group

Library of Congress Cataloging-in-Publication Data

Pearce, Q. L. (Querida Lee)
    The science almanac for kids / by Q. L. Pearce ; illustrated by
Mary Bryson and Mary Ann Fraser.
       p.   cm.
    Includes index.
    Summary: Provides facts, definitions, biographical profiles,
simple experiments, charts, maps, illustrations, photographs,
and tables for ten major branches of science.
    ISBN 1-56565-683-0 (hardcover). — ISBN 1-56565-684-9 (pbk.)
    1. Science—Miscellanea—Juvenile literature.   [1. Science
—Miscellanea.]   I. Bryson, Mary, ill. II. Fraser, Mary Ann, ill.
III. Title.
Q173.P33 1998
500—dc2l

98-25061
CIP
AC

This edition published 1998 by Lowell House
A division of NTC/Contemporary Publishing Group, Inc.
4255 West Touhy Avenue, Lincolnwood (Chicago), Illinois 60646-1975 U.S.A.
Copyright © 1998, 1993 by NTC/Contemporary Publishing Group, Inc.

Printed and bound in the United States of America

10 9 8 7 6 5 4 3 2 1

Managing Director and Publisher: Jack Artenstein
Director of Publishing Services: Rena Copperman
Editorial Director, Juvenile: Brenda Pope-Ostrow
Director of Juvenile Development: Amy Downing
Director of Art Production: Bret Perry
Project Editor: Lisa Melton
Designer: Brenda Leach

Illustration credits:
Mary Bryson—pages 8, 9, 10, 12, 13, 14, 15, 17, 19, 20, 21, 22, 23, 24, 25, 26, 29, 30, 33, 36, 37, 39, 40, 41, 42, 43, 45, 46, 63, 64, 65, 66, 67, 68, 69, 99, 101, 102, 103, 104, 105, 107, 108, 109
Mary Ann Fraser—pages 51, 52, 53, 54, 55, 56, 58, 59, 60, 72, 73, 74, 76, 77, 79, 82, 83, 84, 88, 89, 90, 91, 92, 93, 94

Photo credits:
Dennis Sheridan—pages 16, 18, 27, 33, 34, 37, 38, 45, 49, 52, 57, 61, 70, 71, 72, 75, 76, 77, 78, 80, 84, 85
National Aeronautics and Space Administration (NASA)—pages 6, 115, 117 (Earth), 123
© Anglo-Australian Telescope Board—page 111
© Finley Holiday Film—page 118
© Jim Zuckerman/West Light—cover (lightning)
Pat Riley—page 32
Ann Bogart—page 97

CONTENTS

This book is dedicated to all of the scientists and teachers, such as those listed below, who are committed to making the world of science accessible to children. They are opening the door to the future.

—Q.L.P.

Endorsers:

Zoology: Michael Dee, Curator of Mammals, Los Angeles Zoo

Botany, Ecology & Hydrology: Mycol Doyle, Ph.D., Professor of Botany, University of Maine, Farmington, Maine

Atmospheric Sciences: Michael Ghil, Ph.D., Professor of Atmospheric Sciences and Director, Institute of Geophysics and Planetary Physics, University of California, Los Angeles

Astronomy: Alan Harris, Ph.D., Supervisor of the Earth and Planetary Physics Group, Jet Propulsion Laboratory, Pasadena, California

Physics: Jerome Luine, Ph.D., Staff Scientist, Space and Electronics Research Center, TRW, Redondo Beach, California

Chemistry & Human Physiology: William F. Pearce, Ph.D., Professor of Physiology, Loma Linda Medical School, Loma Linda, California

Earth Sciences: Laurie Reed, consultant, Department of Earth and Space Sciences, University of California, Los Angeles

THE SCIENCES

- *How many bones are there in the human body?*
- *What is a black hole?*
- *What famous scientist studies chimpanzees in Tanzania, Africa?*

The answers to these and hundreds of other fascinating science questions lie in the pages of *The Science Almanac for Kids*. The almanac provides information on ten major branches of science. Each chapter gives an overview of the sciences and includes fascinating facts, definitions of commonly used words, biographical profiles, simple experiments, charts, maps, illustrations, photographs, and tables. In addition, there is an index at the back of the book, as well as an appendix that includes charts on units of measure and the system scientists use to name living things.

Science is the study of the world around us, the universe beyond our world, and the laws that govern it. At this very moment, scientists are making wonderful discoveries about space, our planet, and the living things that populate it. Without a doubt, science is rapidly shaping the world of tomorrow. And science answers many of the questions you may have about your world today.

1

THE PHYSICAL WORLD

And How It Works

Sometimes, when everything appears still and quiet, it may seem that nothing is going on around you. However, the universe is a very busy place. At this moment, no matter how still you try to be, you are moving. Your heart is beating and your blood is flowing. The tiny units called *cells* that make up your body are taking in and burning oxygen to fuel all of your activities. You are also interacting with everything around you. You are breathing in oxygen from the air and breathing out carbon dioxide, absorbing or giving off heat into the atmosphere, and pressing down on the part of the ground where you are sitting or standing.

There are also other things happening around you that you might not notice. For example, Earth's gravity is holding you in place on the planet. That's fortunate, because the Earth is in motion, too, carrying you and everything else on the planet at a dizzying

One of the forces of nature is gravity. Gravity prevents the Earth's atmosphere from escaping into space, and it also traps the moon in orbit around the Earth.

pace in orbit around the sun. Meanwhile, the sun is pouring out energy into space—solar energy that provides us with heat and light.

Energy, such as heat and light, and forces such as gravity are at work in every corner of the universe, and they all appear to obey the same basic laws that govern them here on Earth. *Physics* is the study of those laws. By carefully determining how forces and energy affect objects here at home or in the far reaches of the universe, physicists can predict how the universe will behave. They can also give us a good idea of how our own planet and everything on it works. Finally, the study of physics enables us to figure out how to harness force and energy to run the machines, from computers to cars, that we depend on every day.

Matter and Energy

Although the universe may seem very complicated, it is only made up of two things—matter and energy. *Matter* is any physical thing, solid, liquid, or gas, that takes up space. *Energy* is the ability to do work, or more simply, energy is what makes things happen. For example, the part of the sun you can see is gaseous matter that takes up a lot of space. In contrast, the sun's heat is a form of energy. It doesn't take up space, but it is able to do work, such as make you warm.

Force

A *force* is anything that can cause matter to fall, or that can push or pull matter so that it moves, changes direction, or changes shape. Scientists are always learning new things, but at this time we know about four basic forces in the universe. All other forces are the result of these four. They are the *strong force*, the *weak force*, *electromagnetism*, and *gravity*.

▶ THE STRONG AND WEAK FORCES
The strong force and the weak force act over very tiny distances and affect only tiny bits of matter called **particles** *that are far too small for you to see. In fact, these forces are hardly noticeable over distances greater than a trillionth of an inch!*

The Physical World

Gravity

▶ WHERE THERE IS AIR
On Earth, objects of different weights fall toward the Earth at the same rate. But if you dropped a baseball and a feather from a rooftop at the same time, the baseball would hit the ground first. That is because the air slows falling objects. It slows some, such as light, flat objects, more than others. The moon has no air. On the moon, a feather and a baseball would hit the ground at the same time. Do you think a parachute would work on the moon?

Gravity is a force that attracts every object to every other object so they fall toward each other. If that's true, then why don't you attract things around you like a magnet? Actually, you do, but only very slightly. Gravity is such a weak force that an object has to have a lot of mass (like that of a moon or planet, for example) before the effect of its gravity is easy to detect. The effect also depends on the distance between the two objects involved. The closer they are, the more the objects are likely to fall toward each other.

Earth's gravity causes you to fall toward the center of the Earth. The ground, however, prevents you from falling by pushing up on you. The measure of the force of this push is your *weight*.

field: area over which the effects of a force are felt. The Earth is surrounded by a gravitational field.

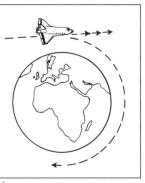

▶ WHAT IS WEIGHTLESSNESS?
A spaceship in orbit high above Earth is actually falling toward the planet. It doesn't crash to the ground because it is also moving very fast horizontally. The astronauts and everything else within the ship is falling, too. This is called **free fall** *because there is nothing to push up on the astronauts and stop their fall, therefore they are weightless. If it were possible for the spacecraft to suddenly stop orbiting and hover in one place, the floor of the ship would stop the astronauts from falling. At that point they would once again have a measurable weight.*

The space shuttle orbits the Earth because it is constantly falling toward it as the ship moves around the planet. Without the pull of Earth's gravity, the space shuttle would fly directly away from the Earth.

Did you know that right now there is about 14 pounds of pressure on every square inch of your body? **Pressure** *is the effect a force has over a given area. Gravity causes the weight of the atmosphere to press down on the surface of the Earth and everything on it, including you. That is called* **atmospheric pressure,** *and it presses down on you at about 14 pounds per square inch.*

Motion

When something falls, it is in motion. *Motion* is any change in the position of an object. Things move only when they are pushed or pulled by a force, or caused to fall by gravity. You could have the fastest bicycle in the neighborhood, but it wouldn't go anywhere unless you got on and pushed the pedals!

Friction

Friction is a force that resists motion between two surfaces. This resistance causes some of the energy of the motion to be lost as heat. The brakes on your bike work by friction. When the surface of the brake rubs against the wheel, some of the wheels energy is lost as heat and the wheel slows. The bike finally stops. There is also friction between your bike tire and the road. That is why if you stop pedaling, you will eventually slow down and stop.

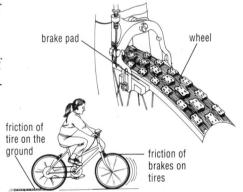

brake pad   wheel

friction of tire on the ground

friction of brakes on tires

ACTION AND REACTION

When you walk, your feet push against the ground. The ground also pushes up against your feet. Otherwise, you would sink. This is one of the laws of motion—for every action, there is an equal and opposite reaction. This is the principle that is used for launching a spacecraft. The blast of gas shooting downward from the tail of the launch rocket causes the craft to shoot upward into the air.

reaction

action

Electromagnetism

Electromagnetism is at work all around you in motors and generators that produce electricity. As you might guess from its name, electromagnetism is a partnership of two phenomena, *electricity* and *magnetism*.

The Physical World

Push Me Pull You

Charge is best explained by describing its effects. When something has a negative charge, it repels (or pushes away) other things that also have a negative charge. It attracts (or pulls) things that have a positive charge. In other words, opposites attract.

You Will Need:
▲ two balloons ▲ a wool sweater or scarf ▲ string

1. Blow up both balloons and knot the ends. Attach each to about a foot of string.

2. Holding the balloons by the ends of their strings, touch the balloons together. They won't repel each other because the atoms in the balloons have equal numbers of protons and electrons so their charges cancel each other out.

3. Now rub the balloons on the wool sweater or scarf. By doing this, you are knocking electrons off of atoms in the wool. The electrons "stick" to atoms in the balloons, causing the balloons to become negatively charged.

4. Now repeat step 2. Will the balloons touch or will they repel each other?

What conclusions can you draw from this?

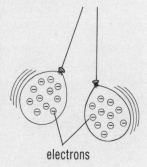

electrons

Electricity

Electricity is a way of sending energy from one place to another. You use electricity every time you turn on a light, use a computer, listen to the radio, or watch television. Electricity runs most of the appliances in your home. Cars also use electricity stored in the battery to help start the engine. Make a list of all the ways you see electricity being used in just one day.

Electricity is the result of a property of matter called *charge*. All matter is made up of very tiny units that you cannot see called *atoms* (see page 25). The atoms are made up of even tinier particles, some of which have an electrical charge. Particles called *electrons* have a negative charge. Particles called *protons* have a positive charge. Most atoms have equal numbers of protons and electrons, so the charges cancel each other out. Atoms that have more electrons than protons are said to be negatively charged. Atoms that have more protons than electrons are said to be positively charged.

atom

Electrical Currents

The electricity you use at home is produced in a power station that may be miles away. The station is connected to your home by a network of special wires that can carry electric current. An *electric current* is a flow of charge (usually electrons) all going in the same direction.

Inside of a Flashlight

The electric current travels from one battery to another through metal conductors.

Arrows show the direction the electricity flows.

on/off switch

Current cannot cross this gap.

on   off

The path of a current flowing through a wire is called a *circuit*, but it will only flow if the circuit is complete. If there is a break in the wire, the flow stops. That is how a switch works. A switch usually has in it a small piece of metal, such as copper. When the switch is on, the metal is in place. The circuit is complete and electricity can flow. When you turn the switch off, the piece of metal moves away, causing a break in the circuit.

▶ LEADING THE WAY
If a magnet is allowed to swing freely, it will point north and south. It's easy to see why magnets were among the first instruments used by sailors to chart their courses on the open sea.

Magnetism

People first discovered electricity about 200 years ago. In contrast, people discovered magnetism, a force that can pull iron or steel, several thousand years ago. The ancient Greeks knew that a rock called lodestone attracted iron objects. In fact, the name *magnet* is from the Greek town of Magnesia, where lodestones were found.

Magnet

north pole — south pole

magnetic field lines

A magnet is a solid object that has the property of magnetism. Like charge, magnetism can be attractive or repulsive. The magnetic force is strongest at each end or *pole* of a magnet. A magnet has two poles, north and south. Poles that are alike push each other away. Poles that are different attract each other.

• •
magnetic field: the area around a magnet where its force can be felt.
• •

Electromagnetic Radiation

The partnership between electricity and magnetism makes many things that you use every day work, including motors, telephones, speakers, tape players, and video recorders. Without this partnership, life on Earth would be much more difficult.

Electrical and magnetic waves traveling together through space form one of the four basic forces: *electromagnetic force.* Without this partnership, life on Earth would be impossible.

RECORD SETTERS

Light (or any electromagnetic wave) is the fastest thing known in the universe. It travels at 186,000 miles (297,600 km) per second.

The Physical World

11

Working Together

Science is so exciting because scientists are always learning new things and solving mysteries. Some discoveries, however, can change the world, and the discovery of the relationship between electricity and magnetism was one. At the beginning of the 19th century, scientists learned that when an electric current is flowing, it creates a magnetic field around it. Soon after, another discovery was made that ushered in a new age. If you move a coiled-up wire through a magnetic field, a flow of electric current can be started, or induced, in the wire. Why is that so important? Because it is the way electric motors work and the way generators produce electricity.

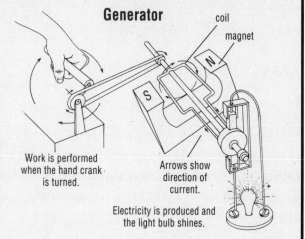

Generator

coil

magnet

N

S

Work is performed when the hand crank is turned.

Arrows show direction of current.

Electricity is produced and the light bulb shines.

▶ MORE ABOUT WAVES

There are a few ways we describe waves of energy. **Wavelength** *is the distance between the peak of one wave and the peak of the next wave.* **Frequency** *is the number of waves that pass by a given point in one second. Frequency is measured in* **hertz.**

Electromagnetic force travels through space in waves of energy. All together, these waves form what is called the *electromagnetic spectrum.* Most of the waves are invisible, but we can see one small part of the electromagnetic spectrum as visible light. Plants use this light energy from the sun to make food and, in one way or another, almost all animal life on Earth relies on plants for food.

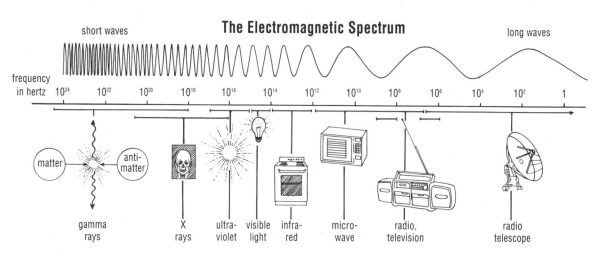

The Electromagnetic Spectrum

short waves

long waves

frequency in hertz 10^{24} 10^{22} 10^{20} 10^{18} 10^{16} 10^{14} 10^{12} 10^{10} 10^8 10^6 10^4 10^2 1

matter

anti-matter

gamma rays

X rays

ultra-violet

visible light

infra-red

micro-wave

radio, television

radio telescope

Light

When you look up at a bright full moon in the night sky, you are looking at sunlight. Some things give off their own light, like a light bulb, a fire, or a television. Objects that give off their own light are called *luminous*. For the most part, the things you see are the result of light rays that are bounced off nonluminous objects. Moonlight is simply sunlight bouncing off the lunar surface.

When light strikes an object, some of it may be absorbed, but some of it bounces off or is *reflected*, just as a ball bounces off a wall. Some of the bounced light reaches your eye. A mirror works because the light waves that are reflect-

reflection

ed, say, from your face are bounced off the surface of the mirror and back in your direction. As a result, you can see yourself, or rather your reflection, in the mirror.

Light can be bent, or *refracted*, too. When light moving through one substance or medium passes into a different medium, it changes speed and is bent in a new direction. You can see an example of this by putting a pencil in a glass of water. The light image of the pencil seems to bend when the light passes from the air into the water.

refraction

Energy and Work

When you are tired and listless, eating a piece of fruit might pep you up. Food is your source of energy. But there are many different types of energy, such as heat, light, electrical, and chemical. Your body stores food as *chemical energy*. Batteries and fuels such as oil, gas, and wood also store chemical energy.

LASERS
Can you imagine cutting through metal, playing music, or performing surgery—all by using a beam of light? A laser *can do all of those things. Light is usually made up of many different wavelengths. Waves of laser light all match each other so the beam is orderly and very narrow. This high-energy beam does not spread out like ordinary light does. As a result, it can cut very precisely. That's why lasers are useful in performing surgery. There is also a laser in every compact disc player. The laser reads the information on the disc. The word* LASER *is short for* **L***ight* **A***mplification by* **S***timulated* **E***mission of* **R***adiation.*

A prism separates visible white light into its component parts: the spectrum of colors.

The Physical World

conduction

convection

radiation

All types of energy can be divided into two groups: *potential energy* (stored energy) and *kinetic energy* (the energy in anything that is moving).

Heating Things Up

Heat energy can keep you warm. It can be useful in other ways, too. Heat can be used to cook food, and hot water is good for washing things. Heat energy is always moving. If you pour yourself a cold drink on a hot day, it doesn't take long before the drink becomes warm. On a cold day, a steaming cup of hot chocolate begins to cool off as soon as it is poured. This is because when two substances (the drink and the air) have different temperatures, heat energy flows from the hotter substance to the cooler one. It flows until both are the same temperature. Heat energy moves in three ways:

conduction—sometimes atoms join together to form units called *molecules* (see page 24). Heat energy is transferred, or conducted, throughout a material one molecule at a time. Heat energy causes molecules to vibrate very quickly. The moving molecules bump into other molecules and cause them to move, too. This continues until all of the molecules in a material are moving.

convection—convection is the way that heat is transferred throughout gases and liquids. For example, in a pot of boiling water on a stove, the water nearest the bottom of the pot heats up first. Because it is warm it expands and becomes lighter than the water above it, so it rises. The cold water then sinks toward the bottom where it is heated, too.

radiation—heat energy moves in waves through the air or through empty space. The waves are called infrared waves, and they are a part of the electromagnetic spectrum. Objects such as the sun radiate infrared waves (among other waves). We feel the infrared waves as heat. An object in the path of infrared rays absorbs the heat energy and warms up. Dark-colored surfaces absorb more heat energy than light ones. That's why you should wear light-colored clothes on a hot day. Shiny surfaces reflect most of the heat energy.

Machines

A machine is anything that can help to do work. Machines also make it possible to do more work with less effort. Here are some simple types of machines:

lever—can be used for moving heavy loads. One end of the lever is wedged under the load. An object called a pivot is placed as close to the load as possible. By pushing down on the raised end of the lever, the load can be moved. Levers are also used to pry things open and to cut things.

inclined plane—sometimes it is easier to slide a heavy load down a slope than to pick it up and lower it. By sliding a load, you get a little help from the force of gravity. When you are lifting a load an inclined plane can be handy, too. For example, it is easier to carry an object, such as a suitcase, when you are walking up a sloping plank than when you are climbing a ladder.

pulley—a simple machine made up of at least one grooved wheel and a rope, chain, or belt. The load is attached to one end of the rope. The rope passes over the grooved wheel, while the other end of the rope is pulled on. It is easier to lift a load with a pulley rather than lifting it straight up because, by pulling down on the rope, your own weight is helping you to lift.

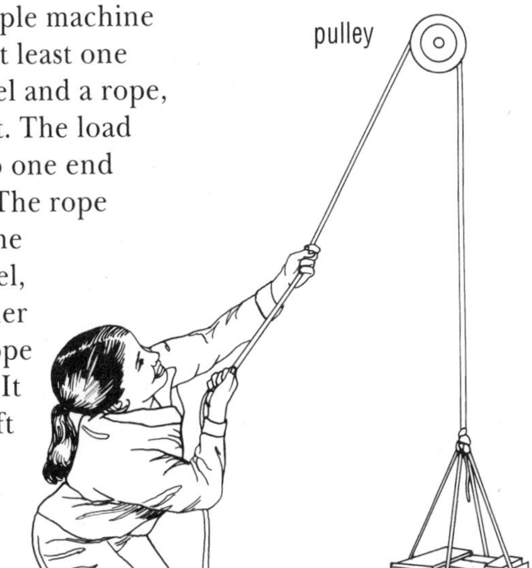

pulley

work: work is what is done when a force moves an object.

The Physical World

15

2

CHEMISTRY

The World of Matter

Matter is anything that takes up space, from a speck of dust or a drop of water to a mighty mountain or a huge ocean. Matter is all around you. The air you breathe, the food you eat, and the water you drink are all matter. Even you are made of matter!

Matter comes in different forms, or *states*. The ground you walk on is solid. Your body, although it might feel solid on the outside, is actually made up of about two-thirds water, a liquid. The air you are breathing at this very moment is a gas. These are all forms of matter.

Chemistry is the study of matter, including the substances known as chemicals that make up different kinds of matter. Chemists study the characteristics of matter and the way different kinds of matter behave or react.

Examples of *chemical reactions*, which are caused by transfers of energy between matter,

New South Wales, Australia: This scene shows the three states of matter—solid (the rocks), liquid (the ocean), and gas (the sky).

aren't hard to find. In fact, there are many going on inside your own body right now. Within your stomach and intestines, food is being digested through chemical reactions. The food you are digesting may have been prepared by cooking, another chemical reaction.

Through the study of chemistry, scientists ask questions about all of the substances that make up our world. For example, will a substance react with other substances? What happens when it is heated or cooled? By answering such questions, chemists can predict how substances will react under different conditions. They can also develop useful new products, from space-age plastics to life-saving medicines.

Describing Matter

Matter can be described in two main ways. It has physical properties and chemical properties.

Physical properties are things we can see or feel but that don't affect the way a material reacts. By contrast, we can't always see or feel *chemical properties*, but they do affect the way a substance reacts. For example, a block of wood is solid. It has measurable size, weight, and appearance. It feels and smells a certain way. These are all physical properties, and no matter how small or in what shape you cut the block of wood, it will still be a block of wood.

If you carve a stump of wood, you are simply *removing* some of the wood. You aren't altering any of the properties of the wood.

But when you set fire to a block of wood, it is likely to continue burning. Through a chemical reaction caused by heat from the fire and oxygen in the air, the wood becomes something else—ash, soot, gas, and heat. Its tendency to burn is a chemical property of wood.

Everything made of matter has *mass.* Mass is how much matter is present in any object. The

When wood burns, its chemical properties change. It is no longer wood, but rather ash, soot, and coals.

17

more matter an object contains, the more massive it is. The mass of something on Earth is measured by finding out its weight, measured in pounds or kilograms. Mass is not the same as *size*, though. If you stood between two life-sized models of yourself, one made of stone and the other a blow-up balloon, you'd be more massive than the balloon, but less massive than the stone statue.

volume: total amount of space anything fills. Volume is a physical characteristic measured in units such as gallons, liters, or cubic feet or meters.

density: measure of how much matter is "contained" in something of a certain size. You can find the density of something by dividing its mass by its volume. You and a stone statue of you may share the same size and volume, but the statue definitely has a greater density!

The States of Matter

Matter can exist in three different physical states—*solid, liquid,* and *gas*—and they are usually easy to tell apart. If you were on one side of a brick wall and a friend was calling out to you from the other side, you would have to walk around the wall to reach your friend. That is because a brick wall is solid. A solid is something that has a definite shape, mass, and volume. The tiny units known as *atoms* that make up the wall are very closely packed. Though they vibrate, they can't move about freely. For that reason, you can't part them and walk through the wall.

Two forms of water can be seen in this view of Athabasca Glacier, Canada—solid ice (the glacier in the distance) and liquid water (the flowing river). What isn't visible (but very much there) is the third form—the water vapor in the air.

A liquid has mass and volume but doesn't have definite shape. It takes the shape of the container it is in. The bonds between atoms in a liquid are not as strong as in a solid. The atoms are still close together, but they are able to move apart more freely. If you were on one side of a swimming pool and your friend called out to you from the other side, you could dive into the water. Though you would feel the push of the water against your body, you would still be able to swim directly toward her.

A gas has mass, but doesn't have a particular shape or volume. Gases simply spread out or take

The Melting Point

All substances have different melting points. You can discover the melting points for some of the things around your home.

You Will Need:
▲ pan for boiling water ▲ tongs ▲ candy thermometer ▲ test items, such as butter, sugar, chocolate, and candle wax (the melting point of metals and glass are too high for this test) ▲ glass test tube or thin glass jar (such as a spice jar)

1. Fill the pan with tap water at room temperature (about 70°F or 21°C) and put the pan on the stove. Turn on the stove to a low setting so the water heats slowly.

2. Place a sample of the substance you are testing in the test tube.

3. Grip the top of the test tube with tongs and lower the tube into the water. Don't let the tube touch the bottom of the pan.

4. With your other hand, hold the thermometer in the water.

5. When the test material begins to melt, check the temperature on the thermometer.

6. Clean the test tube carefully, then repeat steps 2 through 5 for each test material. Your results will be more accurate if you repeat the entire test a second time and then find the *average* temperature at which each substance melted.

the shape of the container they are in. The fast-moving atoms in a gas are very far apart. If your friend called out to you from the other side of an open field, you would feel much less resistance moving through the air to join her than you did moving through the water.

Physical Change

Just because something is a solid, liquid, or gas doesn't mean it has to stay that way. Matter can change in ways you can easily see. Every time it rains, you are seeing liquid water droplets that once rose into the atmosphere in the form of water vapor, a gas. Matter changes its state when something, usually heating or cooling, changes certain of its physical properties. For example, on a warm, sunny day, ice can melt into water, evaporate to become water vapor, condense and form into clouds, then fall back to Earth as solid ice crystals (snow).

Melting

One way substances change state is by *melting* when heat changes a solid to a liquid. Every substance has a particular temperature at which it melts, called its *melting point*. If you have ever tried to eat an ice-cream cone on a warm day, you know its melting point is very low. Water turns from a solid to a liquid at about 32°F (0°C).

At temperatures above 32°F (0°C), ice will melt.

Freezing

Freezing is changing a liquid to a solid. The temperature at which that happens is called the *freezing point*, and it is exactly the same temperature as the melting point. How can that be? Well, that depends on the direction of the temperature. If

Chemistry

At temperatures below 32°F (0°C), water will freeze.

▶ A Shortcut

Substances can change directly from solid to gas without going through a liquid stage. This is called sublimation. Frozen carbon dioxide, also known as dry ice, changes directly from a frozen solid to a gas.

heat is being added, 32°F (0°C) is the melting point at which ice turns to water. If heat is being removed, 32°F (0°C) is the freezing point at which water turns to ice.

Boiling

You can see a liquid turn to gas just by making yourself a cup of tea. When you boil the water, some of it rises from the kettle as steam and invisible water vapor—a gas. *Boiling* is one way to change some substances from liquid to gas. The temperature at which this happens is called the *boiling point.*

Steam is actually water molecules that have evaporated from boiling water.

When water is hot enough—approximately 212°F (100°C)—it boils.

A COOL CUP OF TEA

An increase in pressure raises the boiling point and a decrease lowers it. For example, water usually boils at 212°F (100°C). If you were to climb to the top of Mt. Everest (the world's highest mountain) to make your cup of tea, the water would boil at about 158°F (70°C), because the air pressure at the top of Mt. Everest is much lower than at sea level.

Evaporating and Condensing

When water vapor cools (as it does during the night), it condenses. That's why you see dew on plants and other things during cool, early morning hours.

You don't have to boil water to turn it into a gas. If you put a pie pan filled with water outside on a sunny day, over a few hours the water level will drop. That is because water can slowly turn to vapor, or *evaporate*, at a temperature lower than its boiling point. What happens to the water vapor? As it cools, the water vapor changes back, or *condenses*, into a liquid.

vapor: gas given off from a solid or liquid. Vapors can be cooled or compressed to reform the liquid or solid.

pressure: force applied to or spread over an area. Pressure can be transmitted by solids or by gases and liquids in containers.

Expanding and Contracting

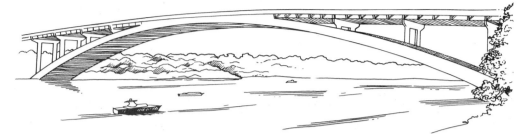

Have you ever watched people on a dance floor? When the music is slow, the couples dance slowly and close together. When the music is fast, the couples dance faster, spread apart, and take up more space. They may even bump into each other. The atoms in substances behave a little like that when temperature changes. In nature, when the temperature is cold, the atoms in a substance move slowly and are close together. The substance *contracts*, or takes up less space. When the temperature is warmer, the atoms move faster and bump into each other. The substance *expands*, or takes up more space. The most notable exception to this, however, is water. It expands when it freezes and contracts when it melts.

Expansion and contraction have to be considered by people who build things like roads and bridges. For example, there are often small gaps left between concrete paving blocks in a bridge to allow for expansion when the blocks heat up.

The concrete blocks in a bridge need small gaps between them so the blocks don't buckle when they expand.

HELPING HAND

You can use the effects of expansion to your benefit. By running hot water over a glass jar with a stuck lid, you can loosen the lid. That is because the metal absorbs the heat and expands faster than glass. By contrast, you must pour hot liquids into a glass slowly because, if the glass expands too rapidly, it can shatter. Putting a metal spoon into a glass while pouring will help. Can you think why that is?

Chemical Changes

An event that either causes a change in the chemical properties of a substance or produces a new substance is called a *chemical reaction*. The substances involved in the changes are called *reactants*.

If you have ever seen an iron tool that has been left out in the rain, you have seen the results of a slow chemical reaction. Iron, water, and oxygen are reactants that produce rust.

Burning is a chemical reaction called *combustion*. When materials such as wood and paper get very hot, they can react with oxygen and burn. The reactants needed for a fire to burn are fuel (such as wood or paper), oxygen, and heat. By eliminating any of these, a fire cannot burn.

product: substance formed or produced by a chemical reaction.

How Does a Car Engine Work?

We use fire to warm our homes and cook our food. Combustion is also an important chemical reaction in everyday life because it is used to power the engines of cars and trucks. In fact, these engines are also known as *internal combustion engines*.

1. The driver turns the key to switch on an electric starter, which causes the pistons in the car's cylinders to move.

2. The pistons move down, drawing in a mixture of air (containing oxygen) and gasoline (fuel) into the cylinders.

3. When the pistons move up, they squeeze the mixture into a smaller space.

4. A spark (heat) from the spark plug in each cylinder causes the gas and air to explode, forcing the piston down again.

5. The up/down movements of the pistons make the crankshaft go around and around.

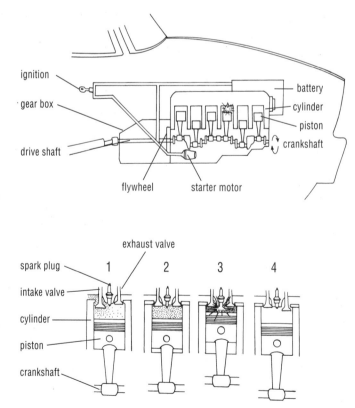

22

6.. The crankshaft turns gears in the gear box, which turns the wheels of the car and makes it move.

rear axle   *differentials*

drive shaft
gear box
crankshaft

Categories of Matter

Matter can be grouped in different categories based on its physical and chemical properties. For example, matter may be an acid or a base, a metal or nonmetal. Different substances can look or act alike in some ways because they share certain characteristics.

Acids and Bases

Have you ever bitten into a lemon? The sour taste can cause your mouth to tingle and your lips may pucker. You are reacting to the acid in the lemon.

A bit of matter called a hydrogen ion is highly reactive with most other substances. Some substances give off hydrogen ions. They are called *acids*. Some substances absorb hydrogen ions. Those are called *bases*.

Weak acids such as lemon juice and vinegar taste sour. Strong acids such as nitric acid can burn and even eat away or destroy metal. Weak bases such as baking soda taste bitter. Strong bases such as ammonia can be dangerous. You should always be very careful when handling any kind of strong acidic or basic substance!

Metals and Nonmetals

Most substances can also be divided into *metals* and *nonmetals*. You can probably find plenty of metals in your own home, such as copper, nickel, zinc, and iron, in the form of plumbing pipes, eating utensils, and much more. Metals are usually natural substances that are dug up from the ground in materials called ores, then purified.

There are many different kinds of metals, but

alloy: substance made of two or more metals or of a metal and a nonmetal. Steel, for example, is an alloy of iron (a metal) and carbon (a nonmetal).

23

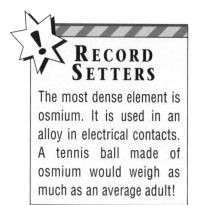
they all have some things in common. Generally, metals are good conductors of electricity and heat (see page 14). With the exception of mercury, metals are solid at room temperature. The most useful property of metals is their strength.

Nonmetals can take many different forms. They may be solid, liquid, or gas, but like metals, they all have some things in common. They are usually poor conductors of electricity and heat, and they also often have low boiling and melting points.

molecule: smallest unit of a compound that can exist on its own and still have the properties of the compound. Molecules can be made of as few as two atoms bonded together or as many as thousands. There are about 600 billion molecules in an average drop of water.

Getting Down to Basics

▶ WHAT'S IN A NAME?
Elements have a chemical name or symbol made up of one or two letters. Compounds are generally described by the elements they contain, and this description can be written as a formula. For example, the molecular formula for water is H_2O, meaning that water is made of two parts hydrogen and one part oxygen.

The simplest element is hydrogen. It is made up of one proton (at center) and one electron.

When you bake a cake you use lots of different ingredients. Each ingredient is a part of the cake, but each is also a separate substance of its own that can't easily be broken down.

Matter is also often made up of different ingredients, but the most basic is the element. An *element* is a substance that cannot be broken down into a simpler substance through a chemical reaction. There are about 109 elements. Ninety-two of them occur naturally on the Earth, and the rest are human made. Elements can be solid, liquid, or gas in their normal state. Helium and oxygen usually exist as gases. Mercury and bromine are elements that are typically liquids. Many of the others are normally solids.

What Is a Compound?

Elements are something like letters of the alphabet—they stand alone. But you can combine letters to make words, and all of the words you use in English are made from the same 26 letters. Similarly, elements can combine to make substances called *compounds*.

A compound is a combination of two or more elements chemically combined. Its properties are different from those of the elements that make it up. The amount of each element in a compound is always the same. For example, water is a compound that is always two parts hydrogen and one part oxygen. Water, of course, is very different from the elements that make it up.

Looking Deeper

Everything is made up of tiny units called *atoms*, which are much too small for you to see. Atoms are so tiny that, if we could magnify one to the size of a Ping Pong ball, a real Ping Pong ball magnified by the same amount would be the size of Earth!

An atom is the smallest unit of an element that still has the chemical properties of that element. Though the word *atom* is from an ancient Greek word meaning "uncuttable," modern scientists have learned the atom can actually be split apart. Atoms are made up of still tinier particles (or *subatomic particles*) called *electrons*, *protons*, and *neutrons*, plus a lot of empty space. The number of each of these subatomic particles determines the type of element a substance is. For example, an atom with one proton and one electron is hydrogen.

If you could see an atom, it might remind you of a tiny solar system. Protons and neutrons are clumped together in the center, or *nucleus*, of the atom. Tiny electrons whirl all around the nucleus at different distances, or levels. Each level is called a *shell*. You might picture the levels or shells around the nucleus of an atom as "parking spaces" for electrons.

When people go to an event such as a football game, they often try to park as close to the stadium (nucleus) as possible. Still, there are only so many places that can be occupied in the row closest to the stadium. Once those places are full, other people have to park in the second row, and so on until all the places are filled.

Parts of an Atom (oxygen)

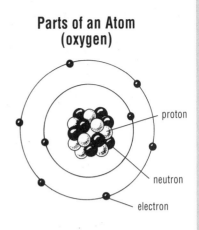

proton

neutron

electron

What a Charge!
Protons and electrons both carry an electric charge. Protons have a positive charge and electrons have a negative charge. Usually, there are the same number of electrons and protons in an atom so the charges cancel each other and the atom is neutral. Neutrons have no charge and their number may be different from the number of protons and electrons.

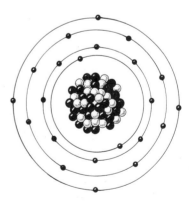

Titanium is a rather large atom, with 26 neutrons, 22 protons, and 22 electrons in 4 shells.

neutrons = ●
protons = ○
electrons = ●

Chemistry

In an atom, only a certain number of electrons can occupy each shell around the nucleus. The first shell can hold one or two electrons. When the first shell is full, any additional electrons must form a second shell. When that shell is full, another one forms. There may be as many as seven electron shells.

The number of electrons in the outermost shell determines how the element reacts with other atoms. The ideal number of electrons in the outermost shell is eight. Atoms that have eight electrons in their outermost shell tend not to react with other atoms. They are called *stable*.

Changing Charge

Atoms usually have the same number of protons and electrons, so they are neutral. An atom that becomes electrically charged by giving off or gaining electrons is called an ion. Atoms that have from one to three electrons in their outermost shell find it easiest to become stable by giving off those electrons. These are ions with a positive charge, because they end up having more protons than electrons.

Atoms with five, six, or seven electrons in their outer shell are closer to having eight if they gain electrons. When they do, the atoms have more electrons than protons and so are negatively charged. This tendency to exchange electrons is the basis for all chemical reactions.

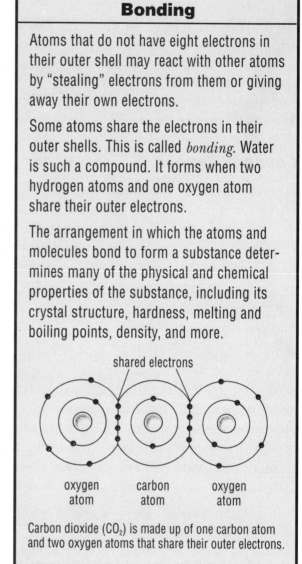

Bonding

Atoms that do not have eight electrons in their outer shell may react with other atoms by "stealing" electrons from them or giving away their own electrons.

Some atoms share the electrons in their outer shells. This is called *bonding*. Water is such a compound. It forms when two hydrogen atoms and one oxygen atom share their outer electrons.

The arrangement in which the atoms and molecules bond to form a substance determines many of the physical and chemical properties of the substance, including its crystal structure, hardness, melting and boiling points, density, and more.

shared electrons

oxygen atom   carbon atom   oxygen atom

Carbon dioxide (CO_2) is made up of one carbon atom and two oxygen atoms that share their outer electrons.

3

EARTH

Our Home Planet

Our Earth is a very special place. Among the planets circling the sun, only Earth is known to support life. That's because of a unique set of circumstances found nowhere else in the solar system. Not only is our planet the right distance from the sun (so it's not too hot or too cold), but it is also the right size for holding onto our precious atmosphere. The atmosphere contains the right mixture of gases needed by living things, and it keeps dangerous solar rays from reaching the surface of our planet. Yet enough heat and light get through the atmosphere to supply the energy living creatures need to survive. Earth also has a plentiful supply of water.

Our planet wasn't always so habitable. If you could climb into a time machine and set the dial back about 4.5 billion years, you would see Earth as a huge ball of rock whirling around the sun. By turning

Over millions of years, the Colorado River carved out one of the United States' great national treasures—the Grand Canyon, in Arizona.

Earth Statistics

age: approximately 4.6 billion years

polar diameter: 7880 miles (12,685 km)

equatorial diameter: 7970 miles (12,830 km)

polar circumference: 24,860 miles (40,010 km)

equatorial circumference: 24,900 miles (40,070 km)

surface area: 196,900,000 square miles (509,971,000 sq km)

average surface temperature: 72°F (22°C)

the dial forward, you could see the incredible changes the Earth has undergone. Over many millions of years, volcanoes would develop as molten rock bubbled up through holes and cracks in the thin crust. You'd watch as gases from the volcanoes billowed out to form an atmosphere. Then rain would begin to fall and oceans would form. After traveling about a billion years, you'd see the very first signs of life in the oceans. Several billion years later, plants would come ashore and life would claim the dry land. Soon after would come the first land animals. As you near the present day, you'd finally recognize your home planet. Even though your journey through time is finished, the changes on Earth haven't ended. *Geology*, which means "Earth knowledge," is the study of our planet and all the changes it is constantly undergoing.

The Earth's Size and Structure

Have you ever heard the saying "you're on solid ground"? The Earth may seem very solid when you're standing on it, but the land beneath your feet is only a very thin *crust* of rock over molten rock many hundreds of miles deep. If Earth were the size of an egg, this hard outer crust would be about the thickness of the egg's shell! Of the two main types of crust, oceanic (under the ocean) and continental (dry land), continental crust is thicker, between 25 and 30 miles (40 to 48 km) thick. Oceanic crust is only about 4 to 5 miles (6 to 8 km) thick!

Below the crust is the mantle, a layer of molten rock called *magma*. Magma has the texture of thick, stiff, gooey, hot fudge and it moves very slowly, about as slowly as your fingernails grow. Below the magma, we finally reach the Earth's core. The core has a liquid outer layer with a solid center that scientists think is probably made up of nickel and iron.

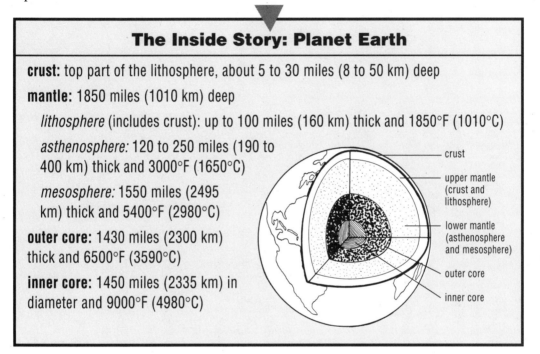

The Inside Story: Planet Earth

crust: top part of the lithosphere, about 5 to 30 miles (8 to 50 km) deep

mantle: 1850 miles (1010 km) deep

lithosphere (includes crust): up to 100 miles (160 km) thick and 1850°F (1010°C)

asthenosphere: 120 to 250 miles (190 to 400 km) thick and 3000°F (1650°C)

mesosphere: 1550 miles (2495 km) thick and 5400°F (2980°C)

outer core: 1430 miles (2300 km) thick and 6500°F (3590°C)

inner core: 1450 miles (2335 km) in diameter and 9000°F (4980°C)

crust

upper mantle (crust and lithosphere)

lower mantle (asthenosphere and mesosphere)

outer core

inner core

The Moving Crust

On a globe or map of the Earth, look at the coastlines of Africa and South America. Don't they look almost like two puzzle pieces that could fit together? That is because they once did! Earth's crust is divided into seven or eight large plates and a dozen or more small plates of moving rock. The plates are much like bumper cars that separate, bump into each other, and slide past each other, at a rate of a few inches a year or less. Perched atop these plates, the *continents* go along for the ride. On average, the plates move no more than about an inch a year.

Earth

The World's Crustal Plates

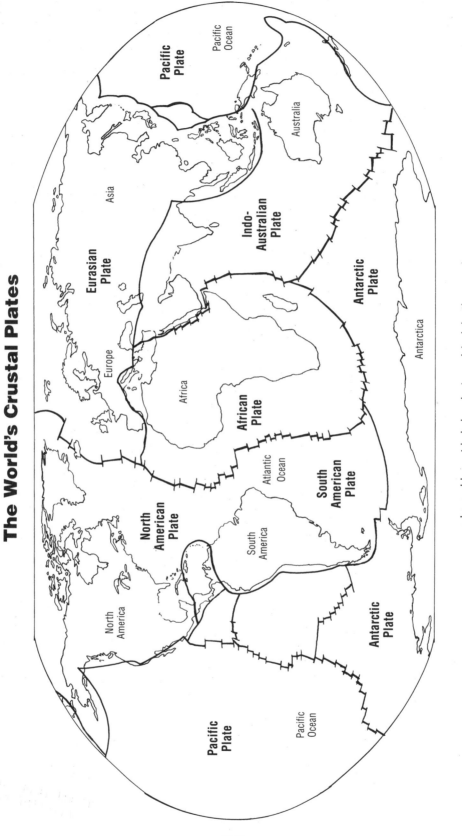

— where old crust is being destroyed (subduction zone)

⊣⊢ where new crust is being formed

Seafloor Spreading

What do you suppose is Earth's longest mountain chain? The Himalayas? The Rocky Mountains? Actually, the longest mountain chain on the planet is underwater. It is a series of huge volcanic ridges that wind beneath the surface of the oceans for about 40,000 miles (64,400 km)! These ocean ridges are found along the boundaries of several pairs of separating oceanic plates. Deep cracks exist along the center of these ridges. Magma from the mantle flows up through these cracks and cools to form a rock called basalt. As new material oozes up, the older material moves outward on each side, like very wide conveyor belts that move the seafloor away from the ridge.

▶ ON THE MOVE

Even as you read this, the Earth's plates are moving very slowly and taking land features along with them. In fact, the pyramids of Egypt are now nearly 3 miles (5 km) farther south than they were when they were first built.

IN PLAIN VIEW

There is a place on dry land where seafloor spreading can be seen at work. Iceland is centered over the northern end of the Mid-Atlantic Ridge in the Atlantic Ocean. As magma flows upward through volcanic vents, the island is slowly growing in size.

Plate Boundaries

Take a piece of cardboard and a piece of paper and move the edges toward each other. When they meet, slide the piece of paper under the cardboard. Earth's crustal plates act something like that. When plates collide, one plate may ride over the other. When an oceanic plate (paper) meets a continental plate (cardboard), the edge of the thinner, denser oceanic plate is shoved downward. Because of the incredible pressure and soaring temperature beneath the Earth's crust, the edge of the oceanic plate slowly dives

HERE TODAY, GONE TOMORROW

Oceanic crust is younger than most continental crust because it is constantly being formed and destroyed. The ocean floor travels from where it forms at an oceanic ridge to where it is destroyed in a trench in less than 200 million years. The oldest rocks on dry land, however, are more than 3 billion years old.

The Scientists

Alfred Wegener
(Germany, 1880–1930)

Alfred Wegener was a German meteorologist. In 1910, he suggested that Africa and South America had once been joined. He proposed that the continents actually drift across the surface of the Earth. Most scientists thought his idea was foolish. Wegener disappeared during an expedition in Greenland in 1930. He never knew that his theory eventually would be proved to be true.

Earth

to destruction and becomes molten magma. This process is called *subduction* and the place where an oceanic plate dives beneath a continental plate is called a *subduction zone*.

fault: weak area in a rock mass. Cracks form along the line of weakness, creating two sections of rock that slip past each other.

Rocks and Minerals

If you were to dig a large hole deep into the ground, it wouldn't be long before you hit solid rock. Earth's crust is made up of rock. The building blocks of rocks are *minerals*. A mineral is a solid material that develops naturally from non-living elements such as carbon, silicon, and iron. Quartz is a very common mineral that develops from silicon.

types of rock

Rocks come in all shapes and sizes, but every rock can be grouped into one of three types according to the way it formed.

igneous rock—formed from molten magma that has cooled and hardened. In fact, the word *igneous* is from the Latin word for "fire." Granite, basalt, and obsidian are igneous rocks.

Sedimentary rock in Grand Canyon National Park, Arizona

sedimentary rock—formed from material worn away from other rocks or from the remains of plants or animal shells. For example, grains of rock worn from a mountain by running water may be carried by the river into the sea and dropped onto the seafloor. That material is called *sediment*. Over thousands of years, the sediment gets thicker as more material is added to it. Slowly the weight of the upper layers squeezes water out of the lower layers. The great pressure helps to cement the material together, forming rock. Limestone, sandstone, and shale are sedimentary rocks.

metamorphic rock—forms when other rocks are changed by great heat or pressure. The word *metamorphic* comes from two Greek words that mean "change of form." The heat and pressure beneath the Earth's surface can change the shape and composition of rocks that are squeezed and folded during mountain building. Marble (formed from limestone) and quartzite (formed from a type of sandstone) are metamorphic rocks.

LONG AGO

Flint is a sedimentary rock that was once used by people to make tools such as axes and scrapers. That's because flint is not only hard, but it can also be chipped to form sharp edges.

Earth Building

You are constantly changing as you grow, but you may not notice any change because it happens just a little bit every day. But if you look at a picture of yourself taken five years ago, you will see a big difference. The Earth is constantly changing, too, but some changes are so slow they are hard to notice.

Mountains

Earth's highest points are the tops of its mountains, but even the tallest peaks were once completely flat. In fact, many millions of years ago, the land high atop Mt. Everest was once at the bottom of an ancient sea! Scientists have actually found fossilized sea creatures on Mt. Everest's slopes.

The Grand Tetons, a mountain range in Wyoming

types of ◄ ·························· mountains

fold mountains—Mt. Everest is part of a huge mountain chain called the Himalayas, in Asia. The Himalayas are examples of *fold mountains*, which form when land at the edge of colliding plates buckles and develops huge folds.

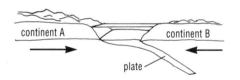

continent A   continent B

plate

continent A   continent B

The plate is destroyed as it is shoved down into the mantle.

plate

volcanic mountains—Earth's tallest mountains are fold mountains, but mountains form in other ways, too. Mt. Fuji in Japan and Mt. Kilimanjaro in Tanzania are examples of *volcanic mountains* that were built up by eruptions of ash and lava.

fault-block mountains—The Sierra Nevada Mountain range of California is an example of a *fault-block mountain range*. It began to form when the land along a lengthy fault was forced upward on one side.

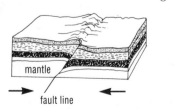

mantle

fault line

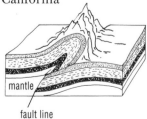

mantle

fault line

Earth

The World's Tallest Mountain Peaks by Continent

Mountain	Continent	Country	Approx. Height (in feet)	(in meters)
McKinley (Denali)	North America	Alaska	20,320	6190
Aconcagua	South America	Argentina	22,830	6960
Kilimanjaro	Africa	Tanzania	19,340	5895
Kosciusko	Australia		7310	2230
Mont Blanc	Europe	France/Italy	15,770	4805
Everest	Asia	Nepal/Tibet	29,030	8850
Vinson Massif	Antarctica		16,865	5140

Tiny Volcanic Island in Crater Lake, Oregon, is unusual in that it formed in the huge caldera of an extinct volcano. That volcano filled with water to form Crater Lake.

Islands

Islands are bodies of land surrounded by water. It usually takes a long time for an island to form. Some islands, such as Greenland and Madagascar, are areas of land that have separated from a nearby continent. These are known as *continental islands* because they are joined to a continent. Other islands, known as *coral islands*, are made up of coral reefs built by tiny sea creatures called coral polyps. The Florida Keys are good examples of coral islands.

Many of the world's islands are the tops of undersea volcanoes. These volcanoes form along

The World's Largest Islands

Island	Ocean Location	Size (in sq mi)	(in sq km)
Greenland	North Atlantic/Arctic	840,000	2,175,600
New Guinea	Pacific	305,000	789,950
Borneo	Pacific	290,000	751,100

mid-ocean ridges and faults. In some places, undersea volcanoes form in the middle of an oceanic plate far away from a ridge. These volcanoes form when oceanic plates move over *hot spots*, areas where pools of magma heat the surface of the Earth's crust. When the crust gets hot enough it thins and the magma rises as a volcano develops.

Violent Change

Have you ever built a sand castle at the seashore? As the tide approaches, the gentle waves may slowly wash the castle away. But one large wave can flatten your creation in the blink of an eye! Some changes on the Earth's surface occur very slowly over time. Others come about quickly— and often violently.

Earthquakes

If you have ever lived in California, you may have experienced a trembling of the Earth called an *earthquake*. Earthquakes occur when masses of rock along a fault in the Earth's crust slip past each other, either horizontally or up and down. As the plates constantly slide, they may hit a "snag" that stops the sliding. This causes stress and pressure

Earth

THE RICHTER SCALE

About 500,000 earthquakes happen every year, but fewer than 100 are strong enough to cause damage. The strength, or **magnitude,** *of an earthquake at its point of origin (called the* **focus***) is measured on the Richter scale, which was developed in 1935. On this scale, each magnitude from 1 to 10 (although it could go higher) represents a quake 32 times more powerful than the number before it. An earthquake of magnitude 5 is moderate. One of magnitude 8 is considered devastating.*

epicenter: point on the surface of the Earth directly above an earthquake's focus.

▶ **A CRACK IN CALIFORNIA**

One of the world's best known faults runs for about 700 miles (1127 km) along much of the length of California. It is called the San Andreas fault. The coastal part of California is moving northward along this fault. If that movement continues, in 50 million years Los Angeles could be far north of where San Francisco is today!

to build up on the rock layers, and the rocks begin to bend. When they finally break loose, ground along the fault line moves very suddenly. A tremendous amount of energy is released and the surrounding area shakes.

Volcanoes

A volcanic explosion can be one of the most violent events on Earth. Can you imagine a mountain belching out fountains and rivers of fiery, molten rock, while spewing dust, gas, ash, and boulders into the air? Fortunately, not all volcanic eruptions are so powerful.

A volcano is an opening in the Earth's crust through which molten rock reaches the surface as lava. They form, for example, near plate boundaries, or at hot spots. In such places, magma can collect in fractures in the crust, or in a pool beneath the ground in an area called a *magma chamber*. In both cases, gas bubbles out of the magma as it nears the surface because it is not under as much pressure as it was when deep within the mantle. When the gas builds to a certain point, the magma is forced upward in an eruption.

types of volcanoes

There are three basic forms of volcanoes:

composite volcano (also called cinder cone volcano)—cone-shaped, steep-sided volcano built up from many eruptions of thick lava, rock, mud, and ash. It has a single opening, or *vent*, in the center.

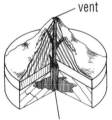

vent

magma pool

fissure volcano—crack in the Earth's surface. Lava may surge out along the entire length of the crack.

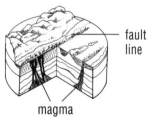

fault line

magma

shield volcano—broad volcano with a curved, rather flattened surface formed from thin, runny lava that erupts fairly continuously over long periods of time. Shield volcanoes generally have more than one vent.

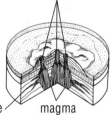

multiple vents

fault line   magma

At the Root of It All

To see if plants can prevent soil erosion, you'll need to prepare this experiment about three weeks in advance. And it is best to set it up outside if possible.

You Will Need:
▲ 2 flat baking pans ▲ soil ▲ box of rye grass seed ▲ aluminum foil ▲ 2 small blocks of wood ▲ watering can

1. Fill both baking pans to the rim with soil. Plant plenty of rye grass seed in one and water it according to the instructions on the box. Keep the pan in a sunny spot. The experiment can continue when the grass has sprouted to an inch tall.

2. Once you have a "lawn" growing, set both pans up with a block of wood under one end so they are tilted. Place aluminum foil at the lower edge of each pan and crimp up the edges to form a catch basin.

3. Water both pans with a half cup of water every day, allowing any extra water to run into the foil. After two weeks, what difference do you see between the two pans? Has the pan with the grass lost less soil?

What conclusions can you draw from this?

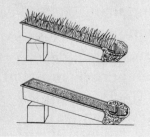

Slow Change

When astronauts landed on the moon, they left footprints in the dust of the moon's surface. If you were to travel to the moon *centuries* from now, you would find those footprints. One reason is because the moon has no atmosphere—no rain to wash away the prints or wind to blow them out of existence. The rocks on the moon today will probably be there centuries from now.

Do you think footprints you make here on Earth will last? How about the rocks you see? Although changes on the Earth's surface can occur very slowly, even the tallest mountains are continuously worn down by two processes that work together: *weathering* and *erosion*.

Water has eroded the side of this cliff at Avila Beach, California.

Weathering and Erosion

weathering: the result of chemical changes occurring in rock, as when the weak acid in rainwater eats away at the minerals in limestone. The minerals dissolve in the rainwater or crumble away.

mechanical breakdown: a type of weathering that results when constant changes in weather cause rocks to crumble into bits or flakes. It can also occur when a plant root forces its way into a crack in a rock, eventually breaking apart the rock.

debris: bits and pieces of rock produced by weathering and erosion.

erosion: the wearing down of land as a result of debris being picked up and carried away by wind, water, or even glaciers. The debris, such as wind-blown sand, can grind away at rocks.

4

THE ATMOSPHERE

Weather and Climate

When you are planning a day at the beach, a picnic in the park, or anything out of doors, it's always a good idea to check the weather report. Today, that's as easy as turning on the television or radio, or reading the morning newspaper to find out if the day will be sunny, or if a storm is expected. It hasn't always been so simple.

Meteorology wasn't recognized as a science until the 17th century. *Meteorology* is the study of Earth's atmosphere and the weather and related events that occur within it. Predicting the weather, or weather forecasting, did not begin until about 1844. It involved a lot of guesswork and was limited to local areas.

Today, scientists gather information about weather patterns with computers, satellites, radar, and many types of equipment that track changes moment by moment. Using communication satellites,

Yellowstone National Park, Wyoming

the information is flashed around the world in an internationally recognized code. When Hurricane Andrew blew through southern Florida and Louisiana in the summer of 1992, people were warned two days in advance of its arrival and so were able to prepare. To gain a better understanding of our global atmosphere and how it works, meteorologists brave the challenge of the icy Antarctic, race after tornadoes, and even fly into the heart of hurricanes.

THAT'S HEAVY !

The total weight of the atmosphere is about 5,000 million million (5,000,000,000,000,000) tons!

Despite newer and newer technology, weather forecasting is complex and it is difficult to predict changes more than five or six days in advance. The more we learn, however, the more accurate forecasts become. This helps farmers who are planning which crops to plant; aids ship and plane navigators trying to plot a safe course; and warns people of oncoming storms. Knowing what the weather holds in store can even help you decide what to wear when you're getting ready for school!

The Atmosphere

Although you can't see it, smell it, or taste it, the atmosphere is all around us. It is a layer of gases (mostly nitrogen and oxygen) that surrounds the Earth. There is also water in the atmosphere in the form of a gas called *water vapor*. The amount varies, but if all the water vapor in Earth's atmosphere fell at once as rain, it would cover the entire planet with a puddle 1 inch (2.54 cm) deep. The air is

Composition of the Atmosphere	
nitrogen	78%
oxygen	21%
argon	less than 1%
carbon dioxide	less than 1%
hydrogen	less than 1%
neon	less than 1%
helium	less than 1%
krypton	less than 1%
xenon	less than 1%

atmospheric pressure: the weight of the air pressing down on Earth. Atmospheric pressure is measured in units called *atmospheres*. One atmosphere is the average weight of a column of air (at sea level) that is 1 inch (2.54 cm) long, 1 inch (2.54 cm) wide, and roughly 300 miles (about 480 km) high (all the way to the upper limit of Earth's atmosphere)! This works out to be about 14.7 pounds per square inch. Atmospheric pressure, however, becomes less the higher above sea level you go.

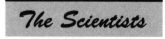
Galileo Galilei
(Italy, 1564–1642)

Galileo made important contributions in many areas of science. In his investigations of the atmosphere, he showed through experimentation that air had weight.

also filled with tiny solid particles, such as dust, ash, and salt.

The atmosphere helps shield the surface of the Earth from dangerous radiaton from space. Acting much like a protective blanket, the atmosphere allows the heat and light from the sun to enter, while shielding the surface from dangerous forms of energy such as ultraviolet or cosmic gamma rays. Without the atmosphere, these rays would destroy most living things on our planet.

The Layers of the Atmosphere

1. troposphere (0 to 10 miles / 0 to 16 km): Most of the Earth's weather occurs within this layer.

2. stratosphere (10 to 30 miles / 16 to 50 km): Most of the atmospheric ozone is found within this layer.

3. mesosphere (30 to 50 miles / 50 to 80 km): The temperature drops quickly in this layer.

4. thermosphere (50 to 300 miles / 80 to 480 km): The air starts to heat up again at this level.

5. exosphere (300 to approximately 600 miles / 480 to 960 km): The outermost layer of the atmosphere. The exosphere is extremely thin and is made up of scattered atoms of hydrogen, oxygen, and helium.

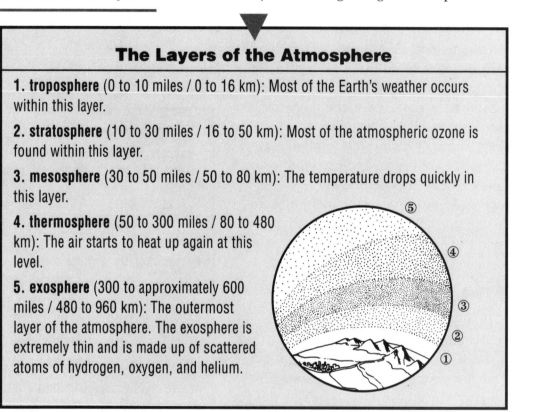

Weather and Climate

▶ **IT'S A FACT!**
If the amount of sunlight reaching the Earth were cut by just 10 percent, the oceans would freeze solid.

Weather is the variety of conditions occurring in the lower atmosphere (the troposphere) at any given place. These conditions include temperature, moisture in the air, and wind speed. Weather can change in hours, or it may stay the same for days or even weeks.

Generally, weather is the result of the movement of huge masses of air of different temperatures.

Heavy Air

Here's a simple way to demonstrate that the air is pushing (exerting pressure) on you and everything around you.

You Will Need:
▲ a full sheet of newspaper ▲ ruler

1. Open the sheet of newspaper and place it flat on a table so its long edge is almost even with the edge of the table.

2. Slip all but about 3 inches of the ruler under the paper.

3. Now try to lift the paper by slapping down on the visible end of the ruler. You'll find that the paper seems to be plastered down to the table!

What's happening?
It's the weight of the air pressing down on the paper that makes it very heavy. In order to lift the sheet easily, press down slowly and gently on the ruler. This allows air to flow *under* the newspaper and so equalize the pressure above and below it.

The boundaries between air masses are unstable and can drift rather suddenly; so weather can change quickly and dramatically from warm and sunny, to cold and stormy, to stages in between.

Climate is the average weather an area experiences over many years. Several things determine the sort of climate a place has. One is how far north or south that place is from the equator. The hottest climates are at or near the equator, and the coldest at or near the poles. Another important ingredient is how high above sea level an area is. The higher you go, the colder it gets. Climate is also affected if the area is mountainous or flat, near the sea or far inland.

Climates of the World

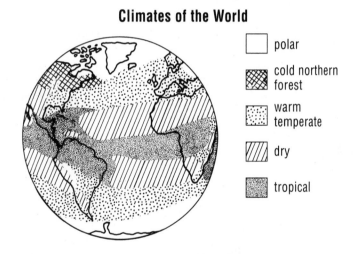

polar

cold northern forest

warm temperate

dry

tropical

▶ IT'S A FACT

The climate can change a lot as you climb a mountain. For example, Mount Kilimanjaro of Africa is located very close to the equator. Its tallest peak, Kibo, is 19,340 feet (5895 m) high. At the base of the mountain the climate is warm and dry. At the top of the mountain there is snow and ice.

air mass: a large volume of air that may be warm, cold, dry, or moist.

front: a boundary between two different air masses.

cold air

warm air

In a warm front, warm air replaces cold air and often brings light rains.

How Do Scientists Predict the Weather?

All around the Earth there are ground-level weather stations equipped with instruments to determine local temperature, wind conditions, rainfall, and other information. Data are also collected by weather balloons and satellites in orbit around the Earth, as well as by radar. All this information is sent to central computers, where it is continuously analyzed by meteorologists. In a single day, the United States National Meteorological Center may analyze more than 100,000 weather reports from around the world!

▶ It's a Fact!

Ocean currents can affect climate on land. Warm or cold ocean currents heat or cool the air above them. As the wind pushes this air toward land, it can alter climate. The city of New York is less than 200 miles (320° km) farther north than the city of Lisbon, Portugal, on the other side of the Atlantic Ocean. However, warm ocean breezes help give Lisbon an average temperature about 20°F (11°C) warmer in winter than New York's.

Wind

Wind is simply moving air. Although storms and gusty winds often affect local areas, there is a huge, fairly predictable worldwide system of air movement fueled by the uneven heating of the Earth by the sun. The hot, steamy equator receives the most direct rays of the sun and the icy, frigid polar regions receive the least. At the equator, warm air rises, moves outward, then cools and sinks again about 2000 miles (3220 km) north and south of the equator, near the areas known as the Tropic of Cancer in the Northern Hemisphere and the Tropic of Capricorn in the Southern Hemisphere. The cool air flows from the two Tropics back toward the equator to complete this cycle.

Earth's Air Patterns

doldrums: belt of calm, low-pressure air near the equator.

trade winds: belt of often fair winds that blow from the Tropics toward the equator, and from east to west in both hemispheres.

horse latitudes: belts of calm winds caused by dense, sinking air, occurring just north and south of the trade winds. At these latitudes on land, most of the great deserts form.

westerlies: mid-latitude winds that blow from about 30 to about 60 degrees north and south of the equator. They flow from west to east.

polar easterlies: where the westerlies meet cold polar air, bands of winds that appear to flow east to west. These polar easterlies are some of the most powerful winds on Earth.

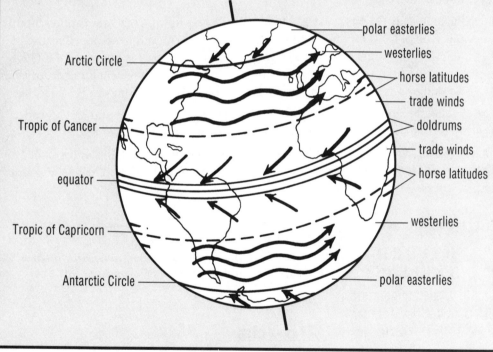

polar easterlies
westerlies
Arctic Circle
horse latitudes
trade winds
doldrums
Tropic of Cancer
trade winds
horse latitudes
equator
Tropic of Capricorn
westerlies
Antarctic Circle
polar easterlies

the Coriolis (kor-ee-O-liss) effect:

The spin of the Earth affects the directions of winds. The Coriolis effect produces a change in the path that each of the Earth's prevailing winds travels. In the Northern Hemisphere the winds swirl to the right and in the Southern Hemisphere they swirl to the left. This effect is named for French scientist Gaspard de Coriolis, who first described it in 1835.

low-pressure area: where the atmospheric pressure is low because warm air is rising.

high-pressure area: where cool air is sinking toward the ground.

▶ IT's A FACT

A sirocco may blow from the Sahara across the Mediterranean Sea to Europe. In 1901, some 2 million tons of desert dust from the Sahara were sprinkled over Europe by the wind. It turned huge areas of snow in the Alps a dull, reddish pink.

▶ winds around the world

Every land has a special name for seasonal winds, from tiny gusts to howling gales. Here are a few:

katabatic winds (Antarctica)—among the most powerful winds on Earth, they may reach frigid gusts of up to 200 miles (320 km) per hour, and blow downslope from the ice sheet toward the sea.

foehn (mountainous regions, such as the Alps)—flowing down from snowcapped mountains, this type of wind is compressed (squeezed together) as it descends. Because of this, a foehn (pronounced FEN) often warms to temperatures as much as 30°F (17°C) higher than the surrounding air. This can be helpful to farmers by helping crops ripen. It can be dangerous, too, since it often causes snow to melt and may cause flooding.

sirocco (Sahara)—powerful, dry wind that builds huge sand dunes and carries red desert dust high into the atmosphere and across the Mediterranean Sea.

chinook (North America, from the Rockies toward the northwestern plains of the United States and Canada)—mild, warm foehn-type wind. It melts snow and brings pleasant temperatures.

RECORD SETTERS

In 1900, the temperature in a town in Montana rose 30°F (17°C) in less than three minutes. The cause? A chinook. The greatest recorded temperature change occurred on a blustery January morning in South Dakota in 1943. The exact cause was not reported, but in two minutes the temperature rose 49°F (27°C)!

THERE SHE BLOWS!

A wind is described by the direction from which it blows. For example, a westerly wind blows from west to east.

Clouds

Clouds are masses of water droplets and ice crystals that form on particles in the air. There are three main types of clouds, and they are categorized according to shape: cirrus, cumulus, and stratus. Scientists have described about ten different combinations of these three main forms. Clouds are also classified according to their height above the ground (measured from the lowest point of the cloud).

Wind River Range, Wyoming

cirrus

cirrocumulus

cirrostratus

altocumulus

altostratus

nimbostratus

stratocumulus

stratus

cumulus

cumulonimbus

types of clouds

The names of clouds come from Latin. These names were given at a time when Latin was the international language of science.

cirrus—highest of the common cloud formations. These delicate wisps are made up entirely of ice crystals. They may signal bad weather.

cirrocumulus—layerlike rippled clouds.

cirrostratus—highest of the layerlike clouds.

altocumulus—cottony rows of gray clouds.

altostratus—thin, filmy gray clouds

nimbostratus—dark gray, layered, low-lying clouds.

stratocumulus—fluffy but patchy gray to white clouds.

stratus—low-lying blanket of gray clouds.

cumulus—fluffy white clouds.

cumulonimbus—towering cloud formed when a warm, rapidly rising column of air meets a layer of cooler air. It is fluffy at the top and flattened below. These clouds often develop into dark thunderheads.

fog: a ground-hugging cloud. Fog generally develops in areas where there are cool temperatures, high moisture content in the air, and only a slight breeze.

Precipitation

Precipitation is moisture in any form that comes from the sky. None of Earth's water vapor escapes or drifts off into space. When it reaches the chilly upper troposphere, rising water vapor condenses to form clouds and the moisture falls to Earth again as precipitation.

some types of precipitation

dew—On a cold, clear morning, have you ever noticed shimmering drops of water on grass, leaves, or even on a spider web? During calm, clear nights, the ground loses heat rapidly. When moist air touches the cold ground or any other cold object, water vapor condenses onto it as dew.

rain—Rain is moisture that falls as liquid drops. In temperate zones, most raindrops begin as ice particles in clouds. When these crystals become heavy enough, they fall toward the ground but melt into raindrops before they reach the surface. In the tropics, water vapor may simply condense into tiny droplets that combine into larger droplets until they are heavy enough to fall.

snowflakes—Snowflakes are collections of ice crystals that usually form within high cirrus clouds. As an ice crystal moves through the air, it sweeps up water vapor and begins to grow until it is heavy enough to fall.

humidity: amount of water vapor in the air.

dew point: temperature at which water vapor in the air condenses into droplets on cool surfaces.

Storms and Special Effects

Sometimes the atmosphere can produce events of spectacular power or delicate beauty.

Tornadoes

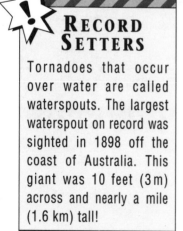

RECORD SETTERS

Tornadoes that occur over water are called waterspouts. The largest waterspout on record was sighted in 1898 off the coast of Australia. This giant was 10 feet (3m) across and nearly a mile (1.6 km) tall!

Nature can sometimes be violent, and certain storms can cause tremendous damage and loss of life. *Tornadoes* are the Earth's fiercest storms. A tornado is a dark funnel of whirling air that hangs from a black thundercloud. Tornadoes form most often where masses of warm moist air and cool dry air meet. Tornado winds may spin as fast as nearly 300 miles (480 km) per hour. If the funnel touches ground, it can inflict tremendous destruction on anything in its path.

Hurricanes

The word *hurricane* is a Carib (West Indian) word that means "big wind." These powerful tropical storms usually develop in late summer over warm ocean waters near the equator. They form when warm, very moist air begins to rise. Surrounding air rushes in to replace the rising air. Winds spin inward toward a calm center of low pressure called the "eye" where there is no wind. When these spinning winds reach speeds of 74 nautical miles (120 km) per hour or more, a hurricane is born. Hurricane winds may reach speeds of nearly 200 miles (320 km) per hour.

Thunderstorms

At this moment, there are nearly 2000 thunderstorms raging in different places over the Earth, and in many of them, *lightning* is blasting from cloud to cloud or from a cloud to the ground. Lightning is a huge electrical spark. Bolts of lightning may reach temperatures hotter than the surface of the sun, and they cause the air around them to expand rapidly. We hear the sound of the expanding air as thunder.

Arcs of Color: Rainbows

Sometimes a combination of sunlight and water vapor in the air can produce displays of fragile beauty. After a rainstorm, if you are standing with the sun low and behind you, you may see a delicate band of color arching across the sky: a rainbow. Rainbows form when sunlight passes through millions of raindrops. The light is bent as it enters each drop, then bent again as it leaves the drop. This bending causes the white sunlight to separate into its seven separate colors. Each color reaches your eye from a slightly different angle and you see a rainbow.

RECORD SETTERS

The greatest annual rainfall occurred in 1861, when 1042 inches (2647 cm) of rain soaked the tiny village of Cherrapunji, India. The average rainfall for that area is at least 425 inches (1080 cm) annually.

▶ IT'S A FACT!
When a single rainbow forms, the order of the colors is always red at the top, then orange, yellow, green, blue, indigo, and violet at the bottom. You may be lucky enough to see a double rainbow. In that case, the order of the colors in the fainter bow is always reversed.

The Atmosphere

Tricks of Light: Mirages

▶ COLD-TEMPERATURE
MIRAGES

*Deserts aren't the only
places where mirages are
found. They occur in cold
places, too. Here's how it
happens: say a ship is sail-
ing in icy waters. Light
reflected from the ship passes through the cold air layer
above the water. When the
light meets the warmer air
layer above, it is bent down-
wards. Because of this,
another image of the ship is
seen in the sky* **above** *the
real ship—a cold-tempera-
ture mirage.*

When can't you believe your own eyes? When you
are looking at a *mirage.* Have you ever seen a distant pool of water across a highway, only to find
the road dry when you reach the spot? The pool of
water was just a mirror of the blue sky—a mirage.

A mirage forms when light is "bent" in the
atmosphere and bounced back to your eye. That
can occur only under very specific conditions.
Gusts of wind usually cause cool and warm air to
constantly mix. Sometimes, though, the cool and
warm air separate into layers. As light passes
through one air layer to another, it is bent toward
the cooler air. In a hot desert, light from the sky
directed toward the heated ground is bent toward
the cooler air layer above. Because of this, light
from the blue sky reaches your eye even though
you are looking at the ground!

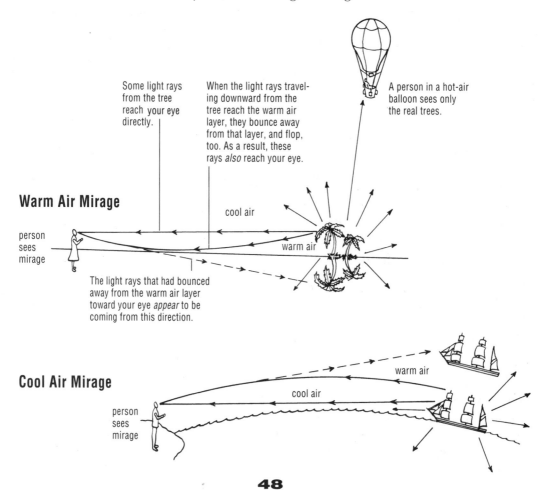

Some light rays from the tree reach your eye directly.

When the light rays travel-ing downward from the tree reach the warm air layer, they bounce away from that layer, and flop, too. As a result, these rays *also* reach your eye.

A person in a hot-air balloon sees only the real trees.

Warm Air Mirage

cool air

person sees mirage

warm air

The light rays that had bounced away from the warm air layer toward your eye *appear* to be coming from this direction.

Cool Air Mirage

warm air

cool air

person sees mirage

WATER

Earth's Great Natural Resource

Try to imagine what it would be like to go through a whole day without water. You couldn't take a shower, brush your teeth, flush the toilet, or wash clothes or dishes, not to mention quench your thirst.

Without water, you also wouldn't be able to eat. For one thing, plants couldn't survive and grow. Consider this: it takes 200 gallons (910 l) of water to produce the single pound of wheat needed to make enough flour to bake a loaf of bread! You wouldn't be able to eat any meat or poultry, either, because the animal the meat came from drank water and probably ate water-loving plants.

On a day without the benefits of water, you may also have to do without things that don't even contain any water. Many of the goods you use throughout a day may have been transported over water, either in ships that crossed the oceans or in river barges. Industries that provide many of the goods you need use water during production to wash materials, or to cool machinery. And, water sometimes is an ingredient in the products themselves.

Fish Falls in Steamboat Springs, Colorado

Water also helps control the Earth's climate. Large ocean currents warmed by the sun at the equator help carry warmth to the colder lands of the world. Cool sea currents can bring relief to hot land areas. Have you ever noticed how a cool ocean breeze can make you more comfortable on a hot day?

Actually, it is impossible for you to go without water even if you wanted to, because there's water in the cells of your body. In fact, you are made up of about two-thirds water.

So although water is the most common compound on Earth, it is very precious and essential to life on our planet. *Hydrology* is the study of the waters of the Earth, including lakes, swamps, rivers, oceans, and even water in the form of ice, such as glaciers.

The Blue Planet

Because water covers as much as 75 percent of the surface of our planet, Earth is often called "the blue planet." Most of this water is in the oceans. The salty taste of ocean water comes from the minerals dissolved in it, which actually came from the land. Runoff from rain, rivers, and streams erodes the minerals from rocks, then washes them into the sea.

Only about three percent of Earth's water is fresh—water that generally contains few minerals, so it can be used for drinking. Much of the fresh water on Earth is frozen as ice at the North Pole and South Pole and so is unusable. That is why it is very important not to waste fresh water or to allow it to become dirty by dumping chemicals or garbage into it.

The Water Cycle

Water never disappears naturally from Earth. Nature recycles, or reuses, every drop over and

Earth's Waters

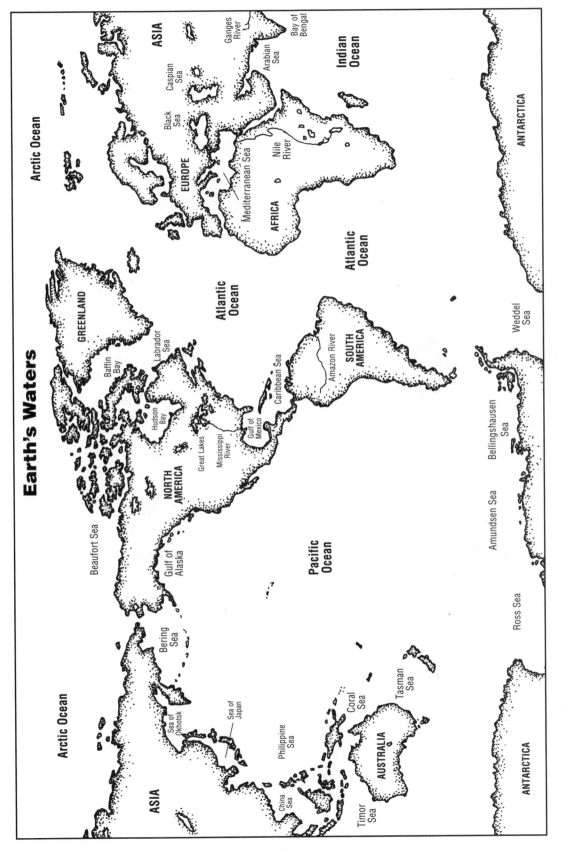

Arctic Ocean

ASIA

Ganges River

Bay of Bengal

Caspian Sea

Arabian Sea

Indian Ocean

Black Sea

EUROPE

Nile River

Mediterranean Sea

AFRICA

ANTARCTICA

Atlantic Ocean

GREENLAND

Baffin Bay

Labrador Sea

Atlantic Ocean

Weddel Sea

Amazon River

SOUTH AMERICA

Caribbean Sea

Hudson Bay

Gulf of Mexico

Great Lakes

Mississippi River

NORTH AMERICA

Bellingshausen Sea

Beaufort Sea

Gulf of Alaska

Pacific Ocean

Amundsen Sea

Bering Sea

Arctic Ocean

ASIA

Sea of Okhotsk

Sea of Japan

Philippine Sea

Coral Sea

Tasman Sea

AUSTRALIA

Ross Sea

China Sea

Timor Sea

ANTARCTICA

Water

The Water Cycle

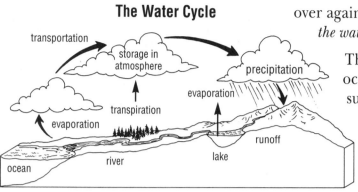

transportation

storage in atmosphere

precipitation

evaporation

transpiration

evaporation

runoff

ocean

river

lake

over again in a huge process called *the water cycle.*

The water cycle begins at the oceans. As the sun warms the surface of the water, the water evaporates and is carried into the atmosphere as vapor. High in the atmosphere it turns cold and condenses into very tiny droplets or freezes into ice crystals. Most of this water returns to the ocean. But part of the water vapor is carried inland on the wind. This is called *transportation.* (Water also enters the atmosphere from sources on land. It evaporates from lakes and rivers, and plants release water from their leaves in a process called *transpiration.*) Water vapor eventually falls as rain or snow, then collects in lakes and rivers or soaks into the soil.

Breaking ocean waves in Montana de Oro, California

The Oceans

You wouldn't enjoy drinking a glass of ocean water, but the oceans are very important to us in many ways. Life on Earth began in the oceans nearly 3.5 billion years ago. The first living creatures were able to survive in the ocean for several reasons. Unlike the atmosphere on land, ocean water provided a stable temperature, and the minerals that early life forms needed were present in the water. The ocean also protected living things

Size and Depth of the World's Oceans					
	Area		**Average Depth**		**Deepest Point**
	(in sq mi)	(in sq km)	(in feet)	(in meters)	(in feet)	(in meters)
Pacific	64,186,300	267,656,870	13,800	4280	35,810	11,100
Atlantic	33,420,000	139,361,400	11,730	3635	31,360	9720
Indian	28,350,500	118,221,585	12,600	3905	23,375	7250
Arctic	5,105,700	21,290,770	3,410	1055	17,880	5545

The Ocean Floor

The average depth of the ocean is about 12,000 feet (3720 m), but the ocean floor has many features that are much shallower or much deeper. Beneath the surface of the water are huge mountains, plateaus, volcanoes, valleys, and deep canyons.

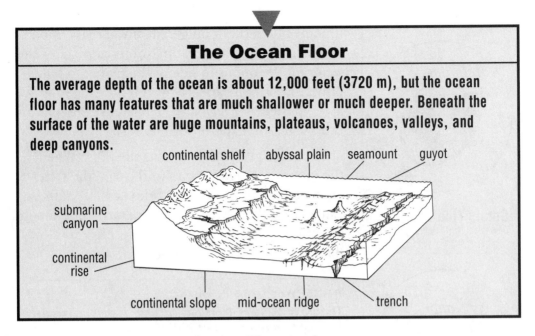

continental shelf   abyssal plain   seamount   guyot

submarine canyon

continental rise

continental slope   mid-ocean ridge   trench

from dangerous rays from the sun. That wasn't true on land because at that time the protective ozone layer in the atmosphere hadn't formed yet. It wasn't until about 400 million years ago that living things, including the very distant ancestors of humans, finally ventured ashore.

People have always relied on the sea for food, such as fish and shellfish, but the oceans have provided another important thing, too. In ancient times, as the human population grew, the oceans became a route to new lands.

The Moving Oceans

The waters of the ocean are never completely still. Many things act on them to keep them moving, including the wind, the whirling of the Earth on its axis (see page 114), and even the effect of the moon's gravity.

The Tides

The oceans rise and fall daily in huge global movements called *tides*. The tides are mainly the result of the effect of the moon's gravity. As it circles the Earth, the moon attracts the water

RECORD SETTERS

The Pacific Ocean is the largest and deepest of Earth's oceans. If you were to drop a marble in a bucket of water, it would reach the bottom in less than a second. If a marble were dropped over the deepest point in the Pacific Ocean, it would take an hour to reach the bottom!

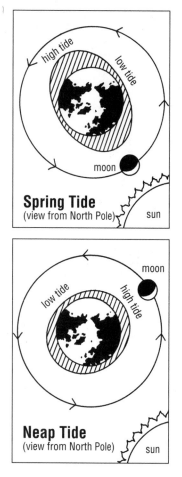

Spring Tide
(view from North Pole)   sun

Neap Tide
(view from North Pole)   sun

upward into a slight bulge. Meanwhile, the force produced by Earth's rotation on its axis causes the water on the opposite side of the planet to bulge outward, too. The areas at which the bulges occur are experiencing *high tides*. The areas between the two bulges are experiencing *low tides*.

The sun's gravity also affects the tides. When the moon is at right angles to the sun, the difference between high and low tides is small. This is called a *neap tide*. When the sun, Earth, and moon are in line, the difference between high and low tides is great. This is called a *spring tide*.

WHICH WAY DOES IT FLOW?
The incredible tides at the Bay of Fundy produce a remarkable sight—a reversing waterfall! At low tide, the waters of the St. John River flow through a gorge and tumble into the bay as a waterfall. That is because the level of the river is somewhat higher than the level of the bay. But at high tide, the bay waters rise higher than the river and pour back through the gorge as a waterfall in the opposite direction!

How Do Waves Form?

Along the coastlines of Hawaii and California, you can often see crowds of surfers in the water. They skim along on colorful surfboards, riding on the crests of fast-moving waves.

An ocean wave is actually energy moving through water. Most waves are created when wind blows across the surface of the water. The energy in the wind is transferred to the water and travels in the form of a wave. The molecules of water themselves move up and down in circles, but not actually forward with the wave. If you watch surfers sitting on their boards waiting for the next ride, you will see that they bob up and down, not forward, when a wave passes by.

▶ TSUNAMI!
The word tsunami is Japanese for "large waves in harbor." A tsunami is a huge wave caused by an underwater disturbance, such as an earthquake, a volcanic eruption, or a landslide. A tsunami may reach heights of 120 feet (37 m) or more.

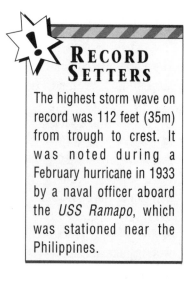

RECORD SETTERS

The highest storm wave on record was 112 feet (35m) from trough to crest. It was noted during a February hurricane in 1933 by a naval officer aboard the *USS Ramapo*, which was stationed near the Philippines.

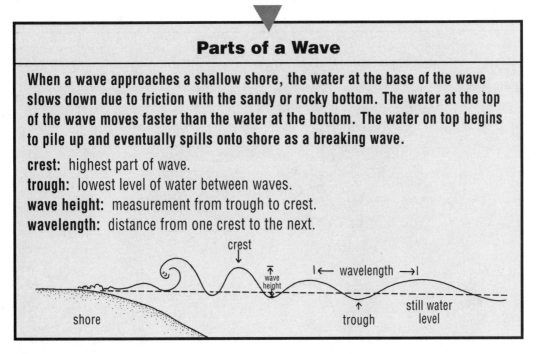

Parts of a Wave

When a wave approaches a shallow shore, the water at the base of the wave slows down due to friction with the sandy or rocky bottom. The water at the top of the wave moves faster than the water at the bottom. The water on top begins to pile up and eventually spills onto shore as a breaking wave.

crest: highest part of wave.
trough: lowest level of water between waves.
wave height: measurement from trough to crest.
wavelength: distance from one crest to the next.

Currents

If you were to blow gently across the surface of a pan of water, you would set a stream of water in motion. As long as you continued to blow, the stream, or *current*, in the pan would continue to flow. Surface currents in the ocean are a little like fast-flowing streams created by the constant, steady, global winds that blow across the water (see the map on page 56). Some currents move slowly at about 6 miles (10 km) a day. Others, such as the Gulf Stream in the Atlantic, may move as rapidly as 100 miles (160 km) in a day.

The Frigid Seas

Temperatures in the ocean vary quite a bit. Shallow, tropical seas may be a comfortable 70°F (21°C) or more. The surface temperature of polar waters hovers near 29°F (–5°C)—and that's in the summer! In winter, icy polar winds lower that temperature enough so that a layer of ice forms, called the *ice pack*. The water below doesn't freeze because the ice pack acts like a blanket that protects the sea from the extremely cold winds. The average thickness of the ice pack is between 8 and 12 feet (2 to 4 m).

MAKING A DIFFERENCE

In winter, the polar seas can freeze over very quickly. In 1989, three gray whales were trapped by the ice off the coast of Alaska. Hundreds of people came to the aid of the trapped whales. Some widened breathing holes in the ice with power saws. Others tried different methods of breaking open an escape route to open water. Sadly, one whale did not survive, but through the unceasing efforts of caring people working together, two of the whales were led to safety.

Water

Ocean Currents

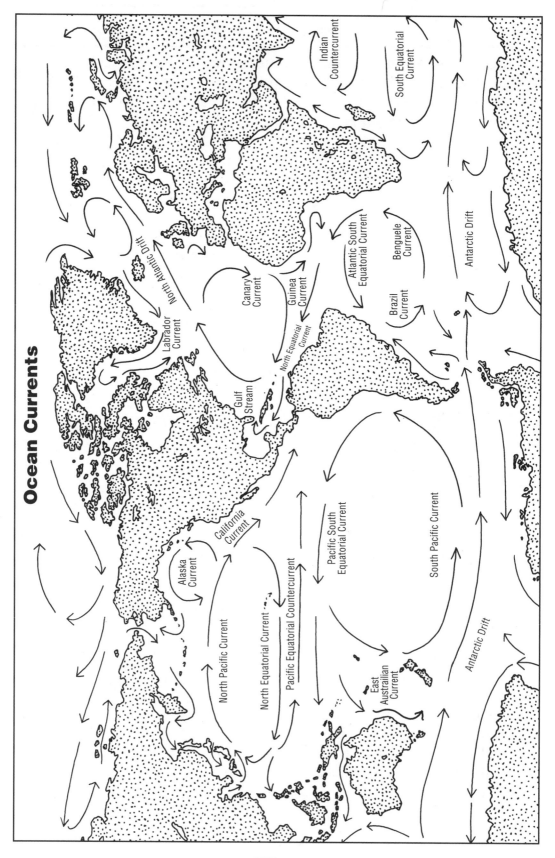

North Atlantic Drift

Labrador Current

Canary Current

Guinea Current

Gulf Stream

North Equatorial Current

Indian Countercurrent

South Equatorial Current

Atlantic South Equatorial Current

Benguela Current

Brazil Current

Antarctic Drift

California Current

Alaska Current

North Pacific Current

North Equatorial Current

Pacific Equatorial Countercurrent

Pacific South Equatorial Current

South Pacific Current

East Australian Current

Antarctic Drift

HANDS ON!

Deep Freeze

Fresh water freezes at 32°F (0°C). Ocean water, however, freezes at about 28°F (–6°C). That's because salt interferes with the freezing process of ocean water and lowers the water's freezing point. You can see this for yourself.

You Will Need:
▲ 2 plastic margarine containers ▲ measuring spoons ▲ salt ▲ marking pen ▲ thermometer

1. Label one plastic container "fresh water" and the other "salt water." Then fill both containers with cool tap water.

2. Now stir 2 teaspoons of salt into the salt water container. Then place both containers in the freezer.

3. Check the temperature of the water in each container every 30 minutes, using the thermometer.

4. Which container freezes first? Does the salt water freeze?

What conclusions can you draw from this?

Fresh Water

People rely on Earth's oceans for food and transportation, but when we are thirsty, only fresh water will do. Fresh water is stored on Earth in rivers, lakes, and in the soil, but most of it is frozen into ice at the poles and on mountaintops.

Glaciers

Glaciers often form high up in mountain gorges, or in places where the winters are very cold and the summers aren't warm enough to melt all the snow. A glacier builds up from tons of snow that have been compressed into ice. Under the force of their own weight, glaciers creep slowly downhill, some just a few inches a day, others many feet.

▶ HAS ANYONE SEEN AN UMBRELLA?
If all the water stored in glaciers were to suddenly evaporate and then fall as rain, the entire Earth would experience a rainstorm that would last for about 50 years.

Mendenhall Glacier, Juneau, Alaska

Rivers

Even the mightiest rivers are often born from small streams of rainwater traveling down mountain slopes, or from underground springs, or the runoff from melting glaciers. Over time, the

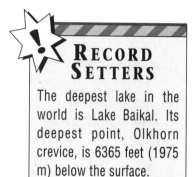
streams carve out a path, called a *bed*, which other streams join along the way. The river grows and steadily makes its way to an outlet in a larger river, a lake, or the sea. In its early stages, a river flows very quickly and erodes away lots of soil and rock to carve a deep V-shaped bed. In the middle stage of its journey, as the riverbed flattens out, the river's flow slows and the bed becomes wider and muddier.

The World's Longest Rivers

River	Location	Length (in miles)	Length (in km)	Outlet
Nile	Africa	4160	6700	Mediterranean Sea
Amazon	South America	4000	6440	Atlantic Ocean
Chang Jiang (Yangtze)	China	3965	6380	East China Sea

Waterfalls

When a river or stream suddenly drops over a ledge or cliff, the result is one of nature's most beautiful sights: a waterfall. One way a waterfall may form is when a river flows over different layers of rock. Some rock layers are harder than others. The rushing water runs across the hard rock with little effect, but eats away at bands of softer rock downriver. When that happens, the level of soft rock lowers, creating a "step" effect.

Cross Section of a Waterfall

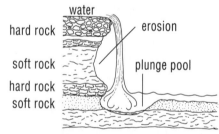

The river water erodes the soft rock.

The World's Tallest Waterfalls

Waterfall	Location	Height (in feet)	Height (in meters)
Angel	Venezuela	3210	995
Southern Mardalsfossen	Norway	2540	785
Yosemite	United States (California)	2425	750

Some falls are the handiwork of glaciers. A moving glacier may creep along the path of a river. As it does so, the glacier carves the riverbed much deeper and wider than the river did. When the glacier retreats, streams that had fed into the original river are now above the new, deeper riverbed. The water in such streams must now tumble over steep drops.

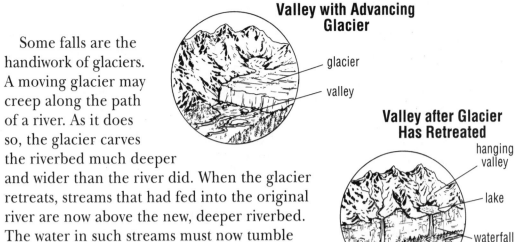

Valley with Advancing Glacier
glacier
valley

Valley after Glacier Has Retreated
hanging valley
lake
waterfall
glacial valley

The World's Largest Lakes

Lakes are inland bodies of water that form when depressions, or low spots, in the Earth fill with water. Lakes may be found in gorged-out valleys, in deep crevices, or even in the openings of extinct volcanoes. They may be fed by streams, springs, or runoff from rain or melting snow.

Lake	Location	Area	
		(in sq mi)	(in sq km)
Caspian Sea (salt)	Asia	143,245	371,000
Lake Superior	North America	31,700	18,705
Victoria	Africa	26,830	69,485
Aral Sea (salt)	Asia	24,905	64,505
Lake Huron	North America	23,000	59,570

Groundwater

How much water do you think might be stored in Earth's lakes, rivers, and swamps? There are about 50,000 cubic miles (208,500 c km) of it. You might be surprised to know that there is *40 times* that amount of fresh water stored in underground rocks! This water is called *groundwater*, and there are about 2 million cubic miles (8,340,000 c km) of it. People who live in areas far from rivers or lakes rely on groundwater from wells or springs as their main source of fresh water.

▶ SOGGY SOIL

One type of groundwater is soil moisture. The soil under your feet is not as tightly packed as you might think. It contains tiny air spaces. Rainwater sinking into the soil fills these air pockets.

water table: highest level, or surface, of an area saturated with groundwater. The level of the water table can change throughout the year.

aquifer: underground layer of sand, gravel, or porous rock that contains water.

▶ WHAT A RELIEF

Aquifers can be thousands of miles wide. In fact, aquifers may stretch all the way from a lush, mountain forest to underneath a desert. In places where the aquifer reaches the surface or where it runs into a wall of impermeable rock, water may bubble up as a cool spring in the middle of the desert—an oasis.

Much of the rainwater that falls on land seeps into rocks below the soil level. It travels downward through rock, such as chalk or limestone. These types of rock are permeable, which means water can pass through them. The water flows around spaces between grains or cracks in the rock. Eventually, it reaches a zone where it is prevented from sinking further by a layer of impermeable rock, such as clay. The permeable rock above becomes saturated with water in a region called the *saturation zone.*

Wetlands—the In-Between Places

Some places, such as swamps, marshes, and bogs, seem to be neither land nor sea nor river. These places are called *wetlands*. Sometimes wetlands can be shallow or even dry. At other times, such as at high tide or during the rainy season, they are flooded with water. Wetlands are extremely important in several ways. To start with, they are key breeding grounds for thousands of types of birds, fish, and other animals. Wetlands such as swamps and marshes are also huge water purification systems. Bacteria and plants growing in them help break down or remove pollutants from the water. Finally, wetlands help control flooding by providing a place where overflow from lakes, rivers, and rain can go.

Cross Section of Land Showing Groundwater

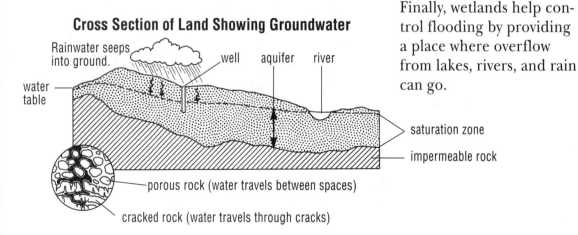

Rainwater seeps into ground.
well   aquifer   river
water table
saturation zone
impermeable rock
porous rock (water travels between spaces)
cracked rock (water travels through cracks)

PLANTS

The World's Food Source

Without green plants, life on Earth could not exist. You may not realize it, but you rely on green plants for food, clothing, and shelter—even for the air you breathe.

Every living thing uses energy from food to fuel its activities, such as growing and moving. Green plants are able to use sunlight to make their *own* food through a process called *photosynthesis*. Animals, however, including people, must depend on plants or plant-eating animals for food.

You might even be *wearing* plant products right now. Cloth such as cotton and linen are made from plants. Look around your home or classroom. How many things can you find that are made from plants? Wood from trees is used not only to build houses and schools, but also to make tables, chairs, desks, and even pencils!

A forest of palm trees, Bali, Indonesia

The Scientists

Gregor Mendel
(Austria, 1822–1884)

Gregor Mendel was curious about how plants pass on traits such as shape and flower color to their offspring. Over many years he raised thousands of pea plants to see which traits were most likely to be passed on. Mendel guessed there were structures inherited from each parent that determined how the young plant looked. He was right, and many years later the structures would be named *genes*.

Plants help to protect the Earth, too. They help to keep the air clean by absorbing carbon dioxide and releasing oxygen—oxygen that animals, including people, need to survive. Plants also send their roots deep into the ground, which prevents precious soil from washing or blowing away. They provide shade, food, and living space for wild animals, too. After considering all these things, it's easy to see why we must protect Earth's plant life.

The branch of science that deals with plants is called *botany*. Botanists study such things as how plants grow and reproduce, where they live, and how they adapt to their surroundings. Botanists provide us with the knowledge we need to keep Earth's garden green!

What Is a Plant?

A plant is a living thing. Like all living things, plants need energy. They must also take in air and eliminate waste, react to changes in their surroundings, and reproduce. But what makes plants different from you and other animals? For one thing, most plants do not have to find and eat their food. Instead, they produce their own food from sunlight, air, and water. There are other differences, too. The smallest part of any living thing is a tiny unit called a cell, and plant cells are very special. Unlike the cells of animals, plant cells have an outer layer, or wall, made up of a tough, supportive material called *cellulose*. Certain plant cells also usually contain *chlorophyll*. Chlorophyll is a substance that can absorb sunlight, which the plant needs to carry out its food-making process, photosynthesis. Chlorophyll absorbs all of the colors in sunlight except green, which is reflected out of the plant. That is why

cellulose: a form of glucose (a sugar). Cellulose makes up the strong cell wall of plants and so ends up being a major part of plant products such as wood and paper.

most plants appear to be green. Finally, plants stay in one place all of their lives. Although they may be able to move certain parts, you won't see a plant pulling itself out of the ground and moving to a new neighborhood!

The Plant Population

Can you guess how many different kinds of plants there are on Earth? Ten thousand? One hundred thousand? Not even close! There are about 300,000 members of the plant kingdom and new kinds are being discovered every year.

The Plant Kingdom

To make them easier to study, members of the plant kingdom are divided into several main groups. The plants in each group share certain features.

Plant Group	Characteristics	Example	Approx. No. of Species
mosses and liverworts	tiny stems; found in damp places	sphagnum moss	25,000
ferns and horsetails	leaves, stems, and roots; live on moist, shady land	staghorn fern	22,000
conifers	woody plants with leaves, stems, and roots; live on land and reproduce by seeds that develop within cones	pine, spruce	800
flowering plants	leaves, stems, and roots; live mostly on land and reproduce by means of flowers and seeds	roses, tulips	250,000

moss   fern   conifer   flowering plant

Plant Highways

The materials you need for this experiment are probably right in your kitchen!

Objective:
to see the xylem in a plant

You Will Need:
▲ a stalk of celery ▲ red food coloring ▲ a tall glass jar

1. Fill the jar with water, add six or seven drops of food coloring, and stir.

2. Cut a straight edge across the bottom of the celery stalk, then set the cut end of the stalk in the water.

3. After an hour or so, take the stalk out of the water, rinse it, then look at the cut end. Can you see the ends of the tiny xylem tubes?

4. Put the celery back in the water. After another hour or so, the leaves will turn reddish as the colored water is transported to them.

What conclusions can you draw from this experiment?

xylem tubes

Parts of a Plant

Plants come in all shapes and sizes, and they have developed many different ways to survive, but most have a few things in common.

The Stem

Just as your backbone supports your body, the plant's stem provides support for its leaves and flowers. The stem stores water and important nutrients. A stem is also the "highway" through which water and sap travel. Tiny tubes in the stem carry the water and sap to all parts of the plant.

• • • • • • • • • • • • • • • • • • • •▶ **parts of the stem**

shoot—new stem.

node—part of the stem from which a leaf and/or buds sprout.

bud—growth on a stem that may become a shoot or a flower.

xylem—network of long, thin tubes that carry water and dissolved minerals from the roots to different parts of the plant.

phloem—network of thin tubes that carry food from the leaves to all parts of the plant.

cambium—layer of cells between the xylem and phloem. These cells divide to produce more xylem and phloem.

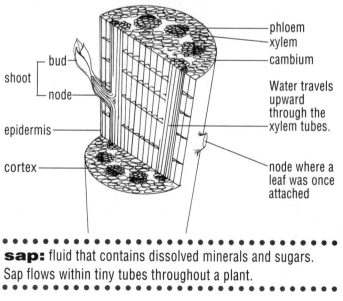

sap: fluid that contains dissolved minerals and sugars. Sap flows within tiny tubes throughout a plant.

epidermis—very thin surface layer around all parts of a plant, including the stem. The epidermis produces a waxy substance that covers its surface and helps to prevent the plant from losing water.

cortex—layer of tissue just below the epidermis. The cortex can store nutrients.

Leaves

When you eat a serving of a leafy plant such as spinach, you are nibbling on a food factory. The leaves of green plants are like efficient factories where sunlight, air, and water are combined to produce the plant's food. But that isn't the only thing that leaves do. Leaves also release gases such as oxygen and water vapor into the air.

RECORD SETTERS

The longest leaves of any plant are those of the raffia palm. A single leaf may be as much as 60 feet (19 m) long!

Plants

The Inside Story: A Leaf

petiole: part of the leaf connecting it to the stem. Some plants have leaves that grow directly from the stem.

epidermis: outermost layer of a plant, including the leaves. The epidermis produces a waxy substance that covers its surface and helps prevent water loss.

veins: food- and water-carrying tubes in the leaf. In many types of leaves there is a central vein called the **midrib**, which branches into smaller veins.

mesophyll: inner layer just below the epidermis. The mesophyll is divided into two layers: the **palisade** and the **spongy**.

stomata (singular–stoma): openings, or pores, found mostly on the underside of leaves. Water and gases (such as carbon dioxide) enter and leave the plant through the stomata.

guard cells: two cells that control the opening and closing of each stoma.

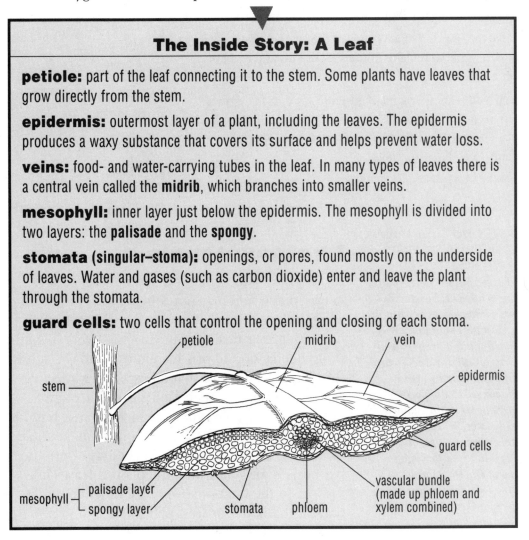

• • • • • • • • • • • • • • • • • • •
transpiration:
loss of water vapor from plants, mostly through the stomata.
• • • • • • • • • • • • • • • • •

Roots

Although you usually can't see them at work, roots are a very important part of most plants. Roots anchor a plant in the soil or onto the branch where the plant is growing. They also draw in the water and dissolved minerals a plant needs to make its food.

• ▶ **types of roots**

fibrous roots—system of roots of equal size. Smaller rootlets branch off from fibrous roots. Wheat has fibrous roots.

tap root—main, central root in plants such as carrots. When you munch on a carrot you are eating a tap root.

adventitious roots—branch out from a stem or a leaf. Strawberries and many grasses have adventitious roots.

aerial root—a kind of adventitious root that does not grow into the soil but remains in the air. Orchids and ivy have aerial roots.

prop roots—another kind of adventitious root that grows out from the stem, trunk, or branch of a tree or other plant, then down into the soil. Prop roots support the plant. Corn has prop roots.

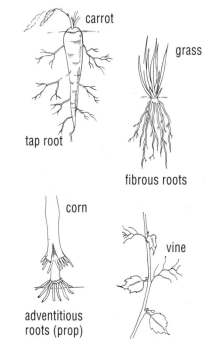

carrot

grass

tap root

fibrous roots

corn

vine

adventitious roots (prop)

adventitious roots (aerial)

▶ **WHY DO SOME PLANTS LOSE THEIR LEAVES IN WINTER?**

Most plants lose and replace leaves all year, but **deciduous** *plants lose every leaf in a short period of time. Why would a plant drop its food factories all at once? To produce food, plants need to absorb several important ingredients—air, sunlight, and water. When the soil is dry or frozen, a plant cannot draw in water through its roots. The leaves are dropped so water already in the plant isn't lost through transpiration.*

Photosynthesis

Do you have a favorite food like hamburgers or maybe pizza? You may not think about it when you are gobbling down a super double cheeseburger, but eating is critical to your survival. Every living thing needs food to provide energy, and the sun is the original source of that energy. But while you can't eat sunlight, green plants can! Through a process called *photosynthesis* (which means "building with light"), plants use sunlight to make their own food. One of the "waste" products of photosynthesis is oxygen, which the plant releases into the air. So the next time you take in a deep breath, thank the nearest plant!

The Photosynthesis Cycle

1. Air containing carbon dioxide enters the plant through the stomata in the leaves.

2. Water from the soil travels through the plant's roots and stems to the leaves.

3. Chlorophyll in the leaves absorbs sunlight.

4. The water breaks up into hydrogen and oxygen, then oxygen is given off to the air through the stomata.

5. Chemical reactions (see page 22) in the plant then produce *glucose*, a simple form of sugar that can either be used immediately as food by the plant, or be converted to starch and stored for later use.

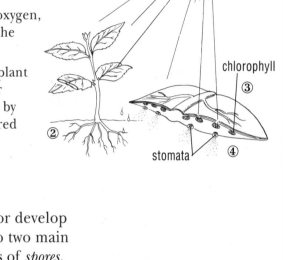

chlorophyll

stomata

Plant Reproduction

Like all living things, plants *reproduce*, or develop new plants. Scientists divide plants into two main groups: those that reproduce by means of *spores*, and those that reproduce by means of seeds. Seed-bearing plants are also divided into two groups, *gymnosperms* (which are mostly cone-bearing plants) and *angiosperms* (which are flowering plants).

Nonflowering plants, such as ferns, horsetails, and club mosses, reproduce by means of small cells called spores. When the spores fall onto moist ground, they sprout into *gametophytes*, which are little structures that have both male and female reproductive cells. When there is enough moisture, the male and female cells join and a new plant grows.

The Life Cycle of a Fern

Sporophyte Development

Gametophyte Development

close-up of underside of leaf, showing sporangia

Each sporangium releases spores into the air.

Each spore develops into a gametophyte.

female cell

egg

The gametophyte plants itself into the ground.

sperm

adult plant

new plant

embryo

fertilization: egg and sperm join

A male cell releases sperm, which swim to an egg in a female cell.

Plants

67

Cones

If you take a walk through a pine forest, you aren't likely to notice spores unless you have brought a microscope along! However, you will probably see plenty of cones. Cone-bearing plants, or *conifers*, are examples of gymnosperms. Conifers reproduce by means of seeds that develop within tough, protective cones.

Flowers

If you stroll through the forest during spring or summer, you are likely to see plenty of flowers, too. Some may be colorful or smell sweet. But flowers are not just decorative, they are a critical part of the reproductive process of many plants. In flowering plants, the first stage of reproduction takes place within the flower.

Some plants produce flowers with both male and female parts, while others have flowers that are either male or female. The male parts of a flower produce tiny grains called *pollen*. The transfer of pollen to the female parts of a flower is called *pollination*. Sometimes pollen may be carried from one plant to another by the wind or water, but there is another very important way that plants are pollinated.

Have you ever watched a honey bee buzz from one colorful flower to the next? The bee is sipping a sweet substance called nectar or dining on pollen. As it eats, the bee brushes against the pollen-bearing parts of the plant. It carries the pollen to the next flowering plant it visits. If the second plant is the same species as the first and ready to receive pollen, pollination occurs. Other animals help to pollinate plants, too, including butterflies, moths, flies, mosquitoes, bats, birds, and rodents.

Once the plant is pollinated, fertilization can take place. Then seeds develop—seeds that can grow into a new plant.

⋯⋯⋯▶ parts of a flower

petals—structures that surround the reproductive parts of a flower and attract birds and insects that pollinate the flower.

stamens—male organs of a flower.

anther—pollen-bearing tip of a stamen.

carpels—female organs of a flower. Carpels are made up of an ovary and a stigma.

ovary—part of a carpel that contains female reproductive cells, or *ovules*, that develop into seeds.

stigma—sticky tip of a carpel.

sepals—the green outermost parts of the flower. The sepals cover and protect a flower bud before it opens.

Cross Section of a Flower

petal
anther
stamen
carpels
sepal
stigma
ovary

fertilization: the joining of male and female cells to form a new cell. Once fertilization takes place, a seed develops that can grow into a new plant.

Plant Survival

Plants are found all over the Earth. They live in your backyard, in the neighborhood park, the oceans, at the bottom of lakes and rivers, and high on mountaintops. Hardy plants also live in some of Earth's most hostile environments—the scorching deserts, and the icy Arctic. Plants have developed many ways to survive in such difficult places.

Snow Survivors

In climates where the weather is always frosty and the ground is often covered with ice and snow, plants have ways of staying warm just as you do

▶ WHERE NO PLANT HAS GONE BEFORE

Although they don't grow there naturally, plants have journeyed into space. A small flowering plant called Arabidopsis *was the very first "astroplant." Because it has a short life cycle of about six weeks, Russian cosmonauts were able to grow it on the Salyut-7 space station in 1982.*

during the cold winter months. Plants on the Arctic tundra are ground-huggers. They never get very tall and so stay out of reach of fierce, frigid winds. Arctic cotton grass grows in tight clumps that protect it from the wind, reducing water loss.

Desert Dwellers

How long do you think you could last in a hot desert without water? Plants need water, too, but in the world's hot deserts, some plants may have to bake in the sun for years without a single drop of rain. Desert plants can survive in this environment because they can conserve water. Cacti are sturdy desert plants that have large, shallow root systems that can absorb water quickly. The water is stored in the plant's stem.

<u>Self-Defense</u>

Have you ever tried to pick a pretty flower and pricked your finger on a thorn? Thorns and spines are one way that plants protect themselves from plant-eating animals. The stems of the octopus tree of Madagascar are studded with rows of spines that are actually longer than its small leaves. The stinging hairs of the stinging nettle have poison sacs at the base of the hairs. An animal that touches the plant not only pricks itself on the sharp hairs, but also gets a stinging dose of the poison as well.

There are even plants that rely on animals to protect them. An "army" of guard ants are often found in the thorns of the bullhorn acacia tree. The tree produces a sweet, sugary nectar on its leaf stalks that the ants eat. In return, the ants patrol the tree and sting any animal that tries to eat its leaves. The ants even chew through the seedlings of other types of plants that may compete with the acacia for space.

A Saguaro cactus, Cabo San Lucas, Mexico

Water Hog

The Saguaro (suh-WAR-uh) cactus of North America has a very widespread root system, and its stems have ridges that can expand. A large Saguaro can soak up and store 1500 gallons (6825 l) of water in a single rainstorm. That is enough to fill three bathtubs—and enough to last the Saguaro for months.

Meat-Eating Plants

Without plants as food, animals would surely not survive. But some plants occasionally turn the tables and have *animals* on their menu!

Meat-eating plants have developed in areas where the soil lacks the nutrients a plant needs. These plants actually trap and eat insects! Once an insect has been captured, the plant releases powerful juices that liquefy the victim so its nutrients can be absorbed by the plant.

Venus's-flytrap

Perhaps the most famous of the "killer plants" is the Venus's-flytrap. Its two-part leaves have tiny hairs on them. When an insect brushes these hairs, it triggers a mechanism that closes the leaf. The jagged edges of the leaf trap the insect in a deadly prison.

Plants as Medicine

You depend on plants for food and shelter, but did you know that plants, even poisonous plants, are a valuable source of medicine? Foxglove is a deadly poison, but very small doses of a substance from the foxglove plant, called digitalis, can help a weak heart to beat more strongly.

Native peoples of the Amazon used to tip their arrows with a deadly substance from certain jungle vines called curare. Scientists, however, have discovered that tiny amounts of a material in curare is a muscle relaxer that can help people suffering from a disease called multiple sclerosis.

Many nonpoisonous plants are used as medicine, too. For centuries, a substance in the bark of the cinchona tree was the only treatment for malaria. It is known as quinine.

Even today, people use many common herbs to treat everything from sleeplessness to colds.

A DEADLY MEAL

Some plants are poisonous to eat. An animal may munch on a few leaves, but then it becomes so sick it avoids the plant from then on. Some plants, such as the foxglove and poison hemlock, have poisons so powerful that they cause a painful death! That is why you should never *eat any part of a wild plant that you don't recognize!*

Plants

7 ANIMALS

Earth's Abundant Family

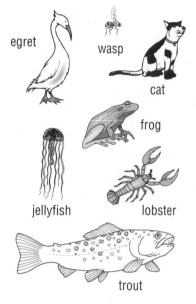

egret

wasp

cat

frog

jellyfish

lobster

trout

No matter where you are on Earth, you are likely to find some member of the animal kingdom sharing your environment. It may be your pet dog or cat, a spider busily building a web in a corner, a bird chirping in a nearby tree, or a worm burrowing through the ground beneath your feet. In fact, humans are also a part of the animal kingdom, so if any friends or family are nearby, you're sharing your environment with animals!

This chameleon from Madagascar is a kind of reptile.

There are many ways that you depend on animals. For example, if it weren't for insects, bats, and birds that pollinate flowers, you wouldn't have various plants to eat. If you eat meat, eggs, honey, cheese, or butter, or drink milk, you are consuming animal products. Some animals, such as certain worms and beetles, act as a natural clean-up crew. They help rid the planet of waste by gobbling garbage and dead plants and animals.

Animals provide clothing, too. The next time you wear a warm, comfortable wool sweater, you can thank a sheep. Some people also wear leather, which is made from the skins of animals. If you have a snugly down comforter or soft down-filled pillows on your bed, you are making use of goose feathers.

Humans have a responsibility to help keep the planet's air and water supply clean for our fellow animals, and to allow them plenty of living space. The study of the animal kingdom is called *zoology*. By learning how animals live and what resources they need to survive, zoologists can help us to find the best ways to fulfill our responsibility.

What Is an Animal?

Animals are living things. They need energy from food to fuel their activities. They must breathe and eliminate waste. Like all living things, animals react to changes in their surroundings, and they reproduce. But what makes animals different from living things such as plants? It isn't just the way they look, because some animals, such as coral and sea anemones, look a lot like plants!

Animals are unlike plants in that they cannot produce their own food from sunlight. Instead, they take in food by eating plants or other animals. Another difference is that animals can move around freely from place to place during all or at least part of their lives.

▶ WHAT IS IT?
*Have you ever seen a drop of pond water through a microscope? A single drop may be filled with dozens of little organisms going about their daily activities. Single-celled organisms called **protozoa** may be tiny, but they can do all of the important things big animals do, including eat, move about, and reproduce. But while some scientists put protozoa in the animal kingdom, others put them into their own special kingdom.*

This amoeba is a kind of protozoa.

Animals

The Animal Population

▶ THAT'S A LOT OF
INSECTS!

A whopping 70 percent of all animals on Earth are insects. And each year, approximately 7000 new species of insects are discovered!

The animal kingdom is broken into two large groups and it is easy to tell which one *you* belong to just by feeling your backbone. The largest group, the *invertebrates*, are animals without backbones (or any bones at all). You belong to the *vertebrate* group, animals with backbones.

The Animal Kingdom

This chart shows the major branches of the animal family.

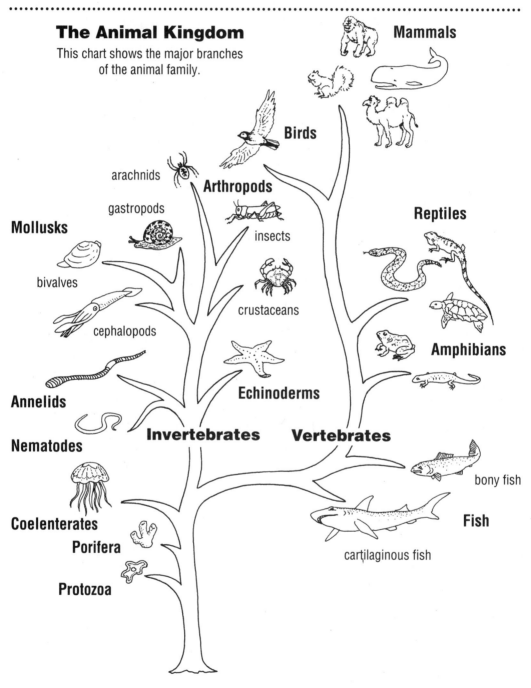

Mammals

Birds

arachnids

Arthropods

gastropods

insects

Mollusks

Reptiles

bivalves

crustaceans

cephalopods

Amphibians

Annelids

Echinoderms

Nematodes

Invertebrates   Vertebrates

bony fish

Coelenterates

Fish

Porifera

cartilaginous fish

Protozoa

HANDS ON!

Bouncy Bones

A mineral called *apatite* makes vertebrate bones strong. You can test this for yourself by removing the apatite.

You Will Need:
▲ 1 cleaned chicken bone (a drumstick works best)
▲ a glass quart jar
▲ household vinegar

1. Fill the jar with vinegar and drop in the cleaned chicken bone.

2. Tightly cap the jar and place it in a cupboard for three or four days.

3. Remove the bone. Rinse and dry it. The vinegar has dissolved the apatite in the bone. Does it feel different than before? What is the result of removing the apatite?

The invertebrate division of the animal kingdom includes an amazing variety of creatures, from jellyfish, sponges, and coral to squid, snails, worms, crabs, spiders, and insects. Some invertebrates, such as worms and jellyfish, have soft bodies. Others, such as clams and snails, have a protective shell. Still others have a hard outer covering called an *exoskeleton*. The exoskeleton provides body support for animals such as an insect, crab, or spider. It also helps protect these

Like all insects, the weevil of New Guinea has an exoskeleton.

animals from the outside environment. Can you imagine what it would be like to have your skeleton on the outside of your body?

Vertebrates, such as reptiles, birds, and mammals, have a strong skeleton of cartilage or bone *inside* their bodies that gives their bodies form and support. The areas where bones meet are called *joints*. Movable joints, such as those in the limbs, allow the skeleton to be flexible. The skeleton also includes a backbone that encloses a bundle of nerves, called the *spinal cord*. The spinal cord connects a vertebrate's brain to other parts of its body (see page 107).

Animals and Food

Do you ever wonder why animals need food? They need it because they use the energy in food to help them grow and move and do all the things they do to stay alive each and every day. Even an animal that is resting is using energy to breathe and regulate the systems in its body. But animals cannot produce their own food. Instead, they eat plants or other animals. Energy from the food passes to the animal that eats it.

A vertebrate's teeth are clues to the type of food it usually eats. For example, even though you may be able to coax your dog into eating unwanted vegetables from your dinner plate, don't let that fool you. Dogs are equipped with the teeth of meat-eaters.

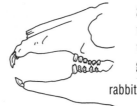
rabbit

Some animals have sharp, flat teeth (incisors) and broad, ridged teeth (molars) for clipping and grinding plants.

Some meat eaters have teeth that are sharp, pointed, and all about the same size. They are for gripping prey. The prey is then torn apart or swallowed whole.

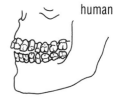
mako shark

dog

Many meat eaters have a combination of teeth for gripping prey and tearing flesh.

The teeth of omnivores are less specialized and are good for cutting, tearing, and grinding plants or meat.

human

A hummingbird's long, thin beak is perfect for sipping nectar from flowers.

Beak Business

Birds do not have teeth. Instead, birds use an extension of the jaw called a *beak* as a feeding tool. The size and shape of a bird's beak can help you figure out what the animal eats. After reading the photo captions, why not take a walk around your own neighborhood and note how many different shapes of bird beaks you can see? Try to guess what type of food each bird eats.

A painted bunting has a short, stout beak for seed crunching.

The upper beak of an eagle is long and sharply curved for eating meat, and it ends in a deadly point that easily rips through flesh.

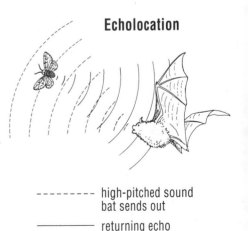

Predator and Prey

A meat-eating animal that hunts, kills, and eats other animals is called a *predator*. Its victim is called its *prey*. Different types of meat eaters have different tools and tactics for finding and capturing their prey. Some, such as the cheetah, use speed to run down a victim. Others, such as the leopard, hide until a prey animal wanders close by, then pounce on it. Predators such as wolves hunt together in groups called packs, and each pack member helps in the capture. Many predators use sharp teeth and claws or beaks and talons to kill. Other tools and tactics are a little more unusual. Here are just a few on the next page.

▶ HEAR, HEAR
Many bats are good at capturing insects. Bats use a kind of radar, called echolocation, to locate their small prey in the dark. First the bat sends out a short, high-pitched sound. The sound bounces off objects in the animal's path. From the returning echo, the bat can figure out what and where the object is.

Echolocation

- - - - - - - high-pitched sound bat sends out
————— returning echo

scavenger: meat-eating animal that does not necessarily kill its own food, but eats the remains of animals that are already dead. A vulture is a scavenger. Some predators, such as lions and hyenas, may also scavenge another predator's meal.

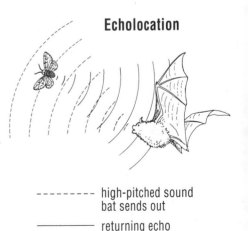

Animals

Tools of the Predator

Tool	Description	Examples of Animals
web	a snare or trap, often made up of sticky strands	spiders
venom	a poisonous liquid, often injected into prey	spiders, snakes
echolocation	a kind of radar	dolphins, bats
electric shock	charges of electricity used to kill prey	electric eel, electric ray
speed	the ability to move as fast or faster than prey	cheetah, falcon
ambush	the ability to hide, then launch a surprise attack	crocodile, leopard
numbers	working together as a group to bring down prey	killer whales, wolves
teeth, beaks, and claws	sharp tools used to rip or pierce flesh	eagle, tiger

Animal Defenses

▶ FAKING IT

Many predators will not eat what they do not kill themselves. For that reason, some animals "play dead" as a form of defense. If an opossum is cornered, for example, it may curl up on the ground and lie perfectly still. Even if the predator nudges the opossum, it doesn't move. Once the enemy leaves, however, the opossum quickly rouses and makes its escape.

As you might guess, many of the tools predators use to capture prey are used for defense, too. Speed is valuable both to catch a meal and to avoid becoming one. A mouthful of sharp teeth, a venomous bite, or an electric shock could easily convince a predator to look elsewhere for a meal.

Some animals are colored or patterned so that they nearly disappear against their background. This is called *camouflage.* An animal that can remain hidden or motionless can use this ability to hide in wait for unsuspecting prey, or to hide itself from a predator.

This leaf insect of Malaysia is a master of disguise.

Temperature Control

Your body works best at a certain temperature level (about 98.2°F to 98.6°F, or about 36.7°C to 37°C). The same is true for all animals. When an animal's body temperature drops below freezing, its cells may actually break apart. If the temperature rises too high—about 113°F (45°C) for most animals—the brain isn't able to work properly.

Most animals, including invertebrates, fish, amphibians, and reptiles, are called cold-blooded. That does not mean their blood is cold. In fact, a desert iguana has a standard body temperature quite close to yours. *Cold-blooded* is a term used to describe an animal that does not control its own body temperature from within. It depends mostly on its surroundings to regulate temperature. When it is very hot out, a cold-blooded animal may hide in a cool, shady spot. When it is very cold, they may stretch out on a warm rock to bask in the sun.

Warm-blooded is a term used to describe an animal that controls its body temperature from within. Birds and mammals, including you, are warm-blooded. When it gets very cold, warm-blooded animals may huddle together or take shelter. Mammals usually have hair or fur to hold in body heat. Birds have down feathers, which are short, fluffy feathers that trap and hold body heat near the bird's skin. If you have ever worn a down jacket, you know how effective these feathers are!

▶ **HOT AND COLD**

Have you ever noticed how you may shiver when you get cold? That is one way your body keeps you warm. Your shivering muscles move very quickly to create heat. When it is hot out, you may sweat. Sweat (water) beads up on the surface of your skin and must absorb heat in order to evaporate. It absorbs heat from your skin and, by doing so, helps to cool you down.

Animals

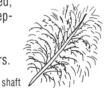

down feather

Birds may be warm-blooded, but they still need help keeping warm. This Greenland white-fronted goose has a thick layer of down feathers.

shaft

migration: long-distance, usually seasonal travel by certain groups of animals, such as birds, between one place and another. Animals migrate when the weather, food supply, or water supply in an area changes.

hibernation: resting or sleeplike state. Animals, such as the ground squirrel, hibernate in winter when food and water may be scarce.

How Animals Sense the World

Have you ever been awakened by a strange noise? That is because no matter how sound asleep you are, your senses are still at work gathering information about your environment. They do this either by sight, hearing, taste, smell, or touch.

Sight

The organs of sight are the eyes. Some animals, such as the jumping spider, have several sets of simple eyes that detect light and dark, or movement. Most insects have compound eyes. They are made up of hundreds or even thousands of tiny *lenses* or sections. What the insect sees through these eyes is a fuzzy pattern unlike the clear picture you see with your eyes.

The eyes of most predators face forward. This arrangement increases the amount of overlap between the two eyes. The overlap makes the animal a better judge of distance because the brain is able to compare two overlapping views of the same picture. This is called *binocular vision*. You have binocular vision. Try covering one eye and reaching out for something a foot or two in front of you. You'll find this easier to do with both eyes open.

The great horned owl's binocular vision and keen hearing help make it a very successful predator.

COULD YOU REPEAT THAT?

An owl can detect a noise one-tenth that of the softest sound a human ear can hear!

Hearing

Many animals rely on their sense of hearing to locate prey or to sense the approach of a predator. An owl, for example, can easily detect the footsteps of a mouse moving across snow or

RECORD SETTERS

The animal with the most eyes is the scallop. It may have as many as 200 tiny eyes lining the opening to its shell.

burrowing through leaves. The owl's hearing is so precise because one ear opening is slightly higher and larger than the other. Sound reaches one ear a split second before the other, allowing the owl to pinpoint the distance and position of the sound's source.

Smell

Have you ever picked up the scent of something good in the oven without even walking into the kitchen? If so, you are using your sense of smell. For a dog, its sense of smell is one of its greatest tools. When hunting, a dog "samples" the air in a series of short, sharp sniffs. Its long snout allows the air to come in contact with many sensory nerves involved with the sense of smell. In fact, some dogs have as many as 220 million nerve cells devoted to detecting smells!

RECORD SETTERS

The world's smelliest animal is the zorilla, an African cousin of the striped skunk. The spray of a zorilla can be detected half a mile away by a human.

How Animals Communicate

When you are happy, there are several ways you might show it. You might smile widely, showing lots of teeth, or laugh out loud. You might jump up and down. Anyone who could see or hear you would know you are happy. Can you think of a way you could tell a dog is happy? What if it wagged its tail? Animals have many ways of communicating with each other, including facial expressions, sound, and scent signals. They use these to send messages of anger, threat, fear, or surrender.

facial expressions—Many animals use facial expressions to communicate. The muscles of a wolf's long snout are capable of a wide range of movement. The animal can show fear, anger, or excitement by changing its facial expression and the position of its ears.

sound—Sound signals are also used to warn or attract other animals. The strange and beautiful moans and calls of the male humpback whale

DO YOU WANT TO DANCE?

When a honey bee finds a good source of food, she hurries back to the hive and does a special dance that directs other bees to the food. This is called the waggle dance. *The direction and number of waggles she makes indicates the direction and distance to the food supply.*

resemble songs. These songs are used to entice possible mates. They can last for up to 30 minutes and be repeated over and over for several hours.

scent—Scent is widely used in the animal kingdom to pass on information. Males of many different species pick out particular hunting territories. A male will fight to defend his chosen territory against any rival male who dares to enter it. As a warning, he regularly marks the borders of his territory with scent signals. Lions and wolves are examples of animals that use urine as the marker. The collared peccary of South America has a scent gland on his back that he rubs against trees and bushes.

How Animals Reproduce

One characteristic of a living thing is that it can reproduce itself, or make a new animal. Some simple animals, such as the hydra, can do this by merely splitting in half. In this case, the new animal is an exact duplicate of its single parent. This is called *asexual reproduction*.

Most animals reproduce by *sexual reproduction*. That means that two parents, a male and female, mate and produce an offspring that shares traits of both parents. Some animals, such as insects, birds, fish, and reptiles, produce eggs. Most mammals give birth to live young.

Insects

Almost all insects lay eggs, but different insects develop from egg to adult in different ways. Insects such as grasshoppers and dragonflies go through a cycle called *incomplete metamorphosis*. There are three stages in incomplete metamorphosis: egg, nymph, and adult.

A Grasshopper's Life Cycle

1. **egg** (in egg mass)

2. **nymph**—the tiny insect that hatches from the egg. The nymph looks similar to its parents, but it does not have wings and cannot reproduce. As it grows, it sheds, or *molts,* its outer layers.

3. **adult**—After time, the nymph develops wings and is able to reproduce. It is an adult.

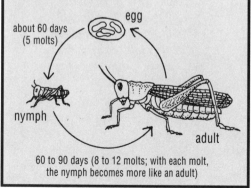

about 60 days (5 molts)

egg

nymph

adult

60 to 90 days (8 to 12 molts; with each molt, the nymph becomes more like an adult)

Insects such as ants, bees, and butterflies go through a cycle called *complete metamorphosis*. The four stages of complete metamorphosis are the egg, larva, pupa, and adult.

Reptiles

Most reptiles lay eggs. Reptile eggs have a protective, leathery shell. Even reptiles that spend most of their lives in water, such as sea turtles, lay their eggs on land. Some snakes and lizards actually give birth to live young.

Amphibians

Amphibians, such as frogs and toads, lay their eggs in water or very damp places. In fact, *amphibian* in Greek means "double life"—and you can see why this name fits. When young amphibians hatch from their eggs, they begin their lives in water, breathing through gills. They then develop legs and lungs and live out much of their adult lives on land.

Birds

It's likely that the eggs you are most familiar with are the hard-shelled eggs of birds. Birds often build a special nest of twigs, grass, or even mud to hold their eggs. At least one of the parent birds and sometimes both care for the eggs and feed the babies after they hatch.

Mammals

An important trait of most mammals is that they give birth to live young. But you may be surprised to learn that some mammals, called *monotremes*, lay eggs. The duck-billed platypus and the echid-

The Monarch Butterfly's Life Cycle

1. **egg**

2. **larva**—In this stage, the hatched larva grows and feeds. The larval stage of a butterfly is called a *caterpillar*.

3. **pupa**—The caterpillar encases itself in a hard covering and begins to change. The pupal stage of a butterfly is called a *chrysalis*. The length of the pupal stage depends on the type of insect and the time of year.

4. **adult**—When the change within the pupa is complete, an adult butterfly emerges, complete with wings.

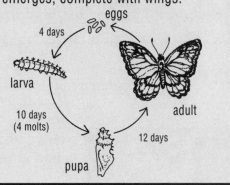

eggs
4 days
larva
10 days (4 molts)
adult
12 days
pupa

RECORD SETTERS

The largest bird egg is that of the ostrich. It may be 6 inches long and weigh more than 3 pounds. A single ostrich egg could hold the contents of 18 chicken eggs!

A Frog's Life Cycle

1 day: The egg is laid in water.

7 days: The tadpole hatches from the egg. The tadpole has a tail and breathes through gills. It attaches itself to a water plant until it is more fully developed.

8 to 10 days: The tadpole begins to swim and eat plants.

7 to 8 weeks: The tadpole develops tiny legs and eats insects. As lungs begin to replace gills, the tadpole gulps air at the surface.

10 to 12 weeks: The tail is absorbed into the tadpole's body and the front legs develop.

12 to 16 weeks: The animal crawls out onto dry land to live out its life as a frog.

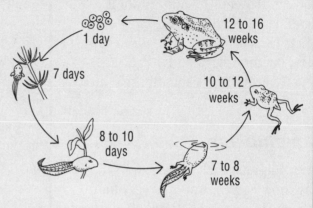

na of Australia are monotremes. They are still mammals, however, because they have fur and the females feed milk to their young. Once the young have hatched, they spend about six weeks in the mother's pouch, which is just a fold in the skin of her belly. The young remain in the pouch until they are old enough to be on their own.

Marsupials are mammals that are born live but are at an early stage in their development. Marsupials include kangaroos, opossums, and koalas. Females have a pouch on their bellies called a *marsupium*. When the young are born, they crawl across the mother's body to her pouch. There, she is able to feed, protect, and care for her young until they develop further and are able to live outside of the pouch.

Most mammals give birth to young that are developed enough to survive away from their mother's body. Called *placental mammals*, they include whales, bears, monkeys, squirrels, and human beings.

The koala of Australia is a kind of marsupial.

ECOLOGY

Our Living Planet

Two important—and very different—environments on Earth are the rain forest and desert.

No matter where you travel on Earth, from the equator to the poles, from the ocean depths to the highest mountaintops, you will find living things. More than 2 million forms of life call this planet home, and you have something in common with all of them. All living things, including you, must share Earth's resources, such as food, air, water, and living space. As a result, all living things are interconnected in complex ways. The study of how living things and their *environment*, or home, affect each other is called *ecology*.

An environment can be big or small. There can even be environments within environments. The Earth itself is our biggest environment. You can think of it

Dinosaur National Monument, Colorado

Daintree Rain Forest, Queensland, Australia

*To get a good idea of just
how complex the interactions
in an ecosystem can be, consider this example of a bee,
a flower, and a tree. The
male euglossina bee of the
Brazilian rain forest uses a
particular orchid as part of
its courtship display to
attract a female bee. If the
orchid were to die out, the
male bees might not be able
to attract females, so fewer
bees would be born and the
species could eventually die
out. If that happened, the
Brazil nut tree would suffer
immensely. Why? Because
the female euglossina bee
pollinates it! Without the
female bee, the tree couldn't
produce new seeds.*

The Scientists

Rachel Carson
(America, 1907–1964)

Rachel Carson was a biologist who had a great concern
for the effects pollution
might have on Earth's natural
environment. Carson's book,
Silent Spring, published in
1962, warned of the long-
term dangers of the careless
use of chemicals to control
insects. *Silent Spring* caused
many people worldwide to
take steps to help preserve
the environment.

as our home in space! But you also live in a tiny
local environment—your house or apartment.

What are the things that can make up a local
environment? If you live in the country, they
might include a forest of trees and shrubs filled
with rabbits, birds, and deer. If you live in a big
city, your local environment might include a
grassy park with pigeons and squirrels. But not
everything in an environment is alive. You
wouldn't last long in a place that didn't have
ground to walk on, water to drink, and air to
breathe! In fact, some of the most important
parts of an environment are nonliving things.
Without sunlight, for instance, plants would not
be able to produce their food. Scientists call all
the living and nonliving things that exist together
in an environment an *ecosystem*. All the things in
an ecosystem are connected in one way or another and give to and take from the ecosystem. By
studying these connections, ecologists can figure
out how resources are being used and what the
results might be when changes in an ecosystem
occur. That is very important because some of
Earth's resources, such as living space and fresh
water, are limited.

The Biosphere

The Earth's largest ecosystem is the *biosphere*. It is
the entire region of the Earth in which living
things can be found, from deep in the ground
where animals and tree roots tunnel, to high in
the air where birds fly. To make the biosphere
easier to study, scientists divide it into smaller
ecosystems called *biomes*.

Biomes

Can you imagine a polar bear living in the
Sahara? Or a camel living in the Arctic? A hot
desert and an Arctic plain are different biomes,
and while the living things of the Sahara must

deal with the heat, those of the Arctic must deal with the cold. Each biome has a particular climate, soil, and plant and animal life. The conditions of each biome are affected by such things as its distance from the equator and its altitude, or height above sea level.

Biomes are broken down into smaller ecosystems, much like your state is organized into smaller cities and towns. And just as there are neighborhoods in your city or town, there are *habitats* within each ecosystem. A habitat is an area where particular plants and animals live. A single habitat may be a large area such as a huge forest. Within that forest there could be hundreds of smaller habitats such as tiny ponds or rotting logs. The group of plants and animals that live in a particular habitat are called the *community*.

The World's Biomes

Listed below are several of the world's major biomes.

cold desert: frozen region of snow and ice with little rainfall (in the form of new snow) and no major land plants.

tundra: cold, windy plain, with low-lying vegetation such as lichens and small shrubs.

coniferous forest: forest of coniferous (cone-bearing) trees, such as spruce and pine, that is cold all year long.

temperate deciduous forest: forest that has cold winters and warm summers and is populated by trees that lose their leaves in winter, such as maple, oak, and beech.

tropical rain forest: warm, wet forest that has a great variety of plants and trees.

steppe and dry grassland: open, grassy plain with hot summers and cold winters.

savanna: grassy plain regularly dotted by trees such as acacia and has hot summers and warm, wet winters.

hot desert: very dry area with little rainfall. Hot days are often followed by cold nights. There is a limited variety of water-conserving plants and few if any trees.

population: group of plants or animals of the same kind or species that live in the same place at the same time. For example, the coast of California has a growing population of sea otters.

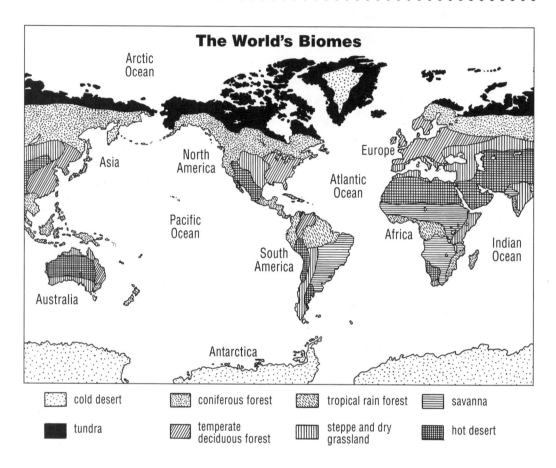

The World's Biomes

Arctic Ocean

Asia

North America

Europe

Atlantic Ocean

Pacific Ocean

Africa

Indian Ocean

South America

Australia

Antarctica

cold desert — coniferous forest — tropical rain forest — savanna

tundra — temperate deciduous forest — steppe and dry grassland — hot desert

Ecosystems

All living and nonliving parts of an ecosystem give to the ecosystem in some ways and take in others. Green plants, for example, take carbon dioxide gas (CO_2) from the air, energy from the sun, and water and nutrients from the soil to manufacture their own food. In turn, the plants give food, shelter, and oxygen to animals. Some animals take from the environment by eating plants, but they also give by pollinating plants or by spreading the plants' seeds. Other animals eat plant-eating animals. And organisms such as bacteria break down dead animals and plants and so help to return important materials, such as carbon, to the soil and air—materials that are used again.

Eco-City

When you think about it, an ecosystem is a lot like an efficient city. For a city to survive, everyone living there must be able to get important goods, such as food and clothing. To supply such things, the city first needs fuel, such as oil and electricity, to provide energy. Factories then use this energy to run machines that make the food and clothing. The factories are the *producers*. Then store owners from all over the city buy the clothes from the factory. The store owners are *primary consumers*. Customers then buy the clothes

Some Habitats in Your Neighborhood

Can you find the plants and animals in each of these habitats?

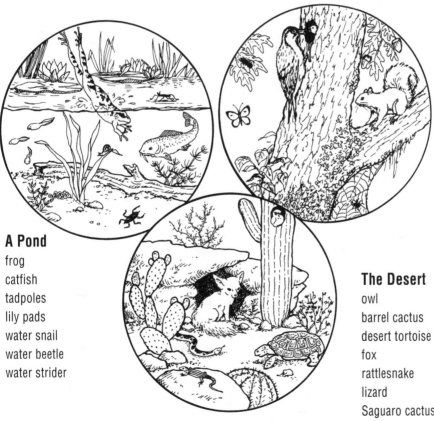

A Tree
woodpecker
squirrel
spider
butterfly
caterpillar
oak tree
lichen

A Pond
frog
catfish
tadpoles
lily pads
water snail
water beetle
water strider

The Desert
owl
barrel cactus
desert tortoise
fox
rattlesnake
lizard
Saguaro cactus

▶ LESS AND LESS

The amount of energy available in food becomes smaller as it moves through a food chain. That is because each animal uses up some of the energy in its food to fuel its daily activities, so there is less to pass along if the animal becomes a meal for another creature.

from the stores, so they can be called *secondary consumers.* When the clothes wear out, they may be sent to a place where they can be broken down and made into something else, or recycled by the *decomposers.*

The energy source of an ecosystem (its "fuel") is the sun. The energy is captured and used by plants. The plants in turn are used as food by consumers. Just as factories are producers of goods purchased by consumers, plants are producers of food eaten by animals. As such, plants are the first link in what is called the *food chain.*

the food chain

first link—Green plants (producers) use light energy from the sun, carbon dioxide from the air, and water and nutrients from the soil to make their own food.

second link—Energy in the plants passes to the next link in the chain—animals that feed on the plants (primary consumers).

third link—Plant-eating animals are eaten by meat-eating animals (secondary consumers), which may in turn be eaten by still other meat eaters (tertiary consumers).

fourth link—Eventually, all plants and animals die and are consumed by such things as worms, insects, fungi, and bacteria (the decomposers). The decomposers are the last link in the chain. They break down dead organisms into simple materials that are finally returned to the soil or air. The materials are eventually absorbed by green plants again. All along the way, energy is transferred from the food that is eaten to the animal eating it.

A Typical Food Chain

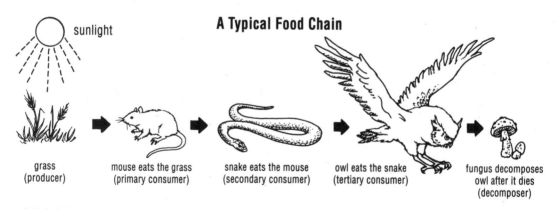

grass (producer) → mouse eats the grass (primary consumer) → snake eats the mouse (secondary consumer) → owl eats the snake (tertiary consumer) → fungus decomposes owl after it dies (decomposer)

growth rate: the difference between the birth and death rates of populations of living things. If more organisms are being born than are dying, the population is growing. If more organisms are dying than being born, the population is decreasing. If the levels are about even, the population's growth rate is stable.

The Nonliving Environment

As we've seen, not everything in an ecosystem is a plant or animal. Air, soil, water, and sunshine are critical to the environment. Carbon is very important, too. This nonliving element is used over and over again in a cycle called the *carbon cycle.*

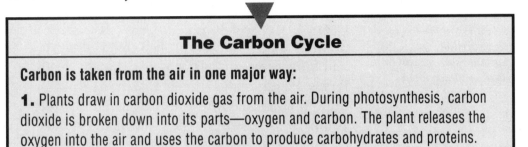

The Carbon Cycle

Carbon is taken from the air in one major way:

1. Plants draw in carbon dioxide gas from the air. During photosynthesis, carbon dioxide is broken down into its parts—oxygen and carbon. The plant releases the oxygen into the air and uses the carbon to produce carbohydrates and proteins.

Carbon returns to the air in several ways:

1. Animals release carbon dioxide gas when they exhale. This process is called *respiration.*

2. When animals eat plants, they take in carbon in the form of carbohydrates and proteins. When an animal dies, decomposers break down its body and release some of the carbon into the air as carbon dioxide gas.

3. Some carbon from dead animals and plants is stored in the soil. Over millions of years, dead organisms may turn into coal and oil. These are called *fossil fuels* because they are the remains of ancient living things. Carbon dioxide is released into the air when humans burn these fossil fuels for energy.

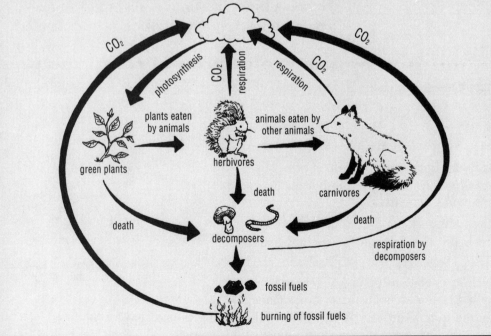

▶ DON'T TREAT IT LIKE
DIRT!

*The formation of a layer of
rich topsoil from bare rock
may take as long as 10,000
years. Plants send their
roots deep into the soil
layer, which helps to keep it
in place. When land is care-
lessly cleared of plants, this
important resource can be
washed or blown away.*

COMMENSALISM

*The remora is a fish with a
special "sucker" on its head
that allows it to attach itself
to a shark. The shark
doesn't gain from this relationship, but it doesn't lose
anything either. The remora,
however, benefits a great
deal. By attaching itself to a
fierce predator, the remora
gains protection from its
own predators. It also gets
to eat scraps from the
shark's meals.*

The Soil

Have you ever planted a garden? If you have, you
know that most plants do not grow well unless
they have good soil. Soil is another important
nonliving part of an ecosystem. *Topsoil* is generally considered to be the upper two feet (61 cm) or
less of a layer of soil. It forms when rock is worn
down by wind and rain, broken up by plant roots
and burrowing animals, and enriched by dead
leaves. Plants anchor their roots in the soil and
draw in water and nutrients through their roots.
Plants are the basis for the food chains in most
ecosystems, so soil is an important nonliving link
in an ecosystem.

Ecosystem Relationships

You interact with many different people in your
life, and you probably act in different ways with
different people. You might behave one way with
your parents, another way with your brothers and
sisters, and still other ways with friends or teachers. All living things must interact with other living things, and they do it in very specific ways.
Here is a list of the kinds of plant and animal
relationships. Can you think of other examples?

plant and animal relationships

competition—Relationship in which living things compete for the same resources, such
as food or shelter.

predation—Capture and use of one animal as food by another
animal. A *predator* hunts, kills, and eats prey.

parasitism—Relationship in which one plant or animal
(the *host*) is harmed, while another plant or animal
(the *parasite*) benefits.

commensalism—Relationship in which one partner benefits, but the other is generally unaffect-
ed.

mutualism—Relationship in which both partners
benefit. Lichens are made up of two organisms,
algae and fungi. Through photosynthesis, the algae produce food for the fungi.
In turn, the fungi give support to the algae and keep them from drying out.

Wolves are predators that hunt and
kill deer and other animals for food.

HANDS ON!

In the Field

Objective:
To learn about your local ecosystem.

You Will Need:
▲ notebook ▲ pencil or pen ▲ camera and/or binoculars (optional)

1. Choose an area you would like to study. An overgrown lot or field, a pond or stream, or a section of woodland would be good.

2. Make careful notes about the conditions in the area, such as the overall weather and the source of water.

3. Note the types of plants that grow in the area. Which plants are dominant (most plentiful)? Which seem scarce?

4. Look for signs of animal life, including insects, birds, and mammals. Don't forget the animals in the soil! Try not to disturb any animals you find.

5. Note any changes in the area over short periods of time, such as changes in the amount of water, which plants have been eaten by animals, or which plants are flowering.

6. Observe the same area during different seasons. You can add to your study by drawing sketches of the plants and animals you see, and by collecting samples, such as bird feathers and leaves, to paste in your notebook.

What conclusions have you drawn from your study?

The Changing Ecosystem

The Earth is always changing. Ecosystems change, too. Ponds dry up. Beaches slowly wash away. Trees and even entire forests die out. Changes can happen quickly, too. A disaster such as a fiery volcanic eruption, a devastating flood, a landslide, or a forest fire can wipe out habitats and destroy whole communities. But, over time, a new community develops. This is called *succession*. The rate of succession is very different for every type of ecosystem, but the sample below will give you an idea of how it works.

Succession After a Forest Fire

1. A forest is destroyed by a fire.

2. Pioneer community (1 to 10 years)—grasses begin to grow. Insects and small rodents return.

3. Successional community (10 to 25 years)—low shrubs and bushes take over. Primary consumers, such as rabbits and seed-eating birds, return as their food supply grows back. Small meat eaters soon follow.

4. Climax community (25 to 100 years)—tall trees take hold. Large plant eaters such as deer return, as do meat eaters such as foxes and owls.

Extinction

When disastrous changes occur in an ecosystem, some populations may *not* return. How would you like to have a pet dinosaur or visit a dinosaur zoo? Unfortunately, these are not possibilities since dinosaurs have not walked the Earth for at least 65 million years. They are *extinct*, or gone forever.

an extinct dinosaur—
Ankylosaurus

Some living things become extinct because they cannot survive changes in their environment. When the climate in an area becomes colder, for example, populations may die out. When a habitat disappears, as when a lake dries up, so might the plants and animals that lived there. Entire species may even die out.

Extinction is usually a natural process. However, people have put many animal and plant populations in serious danger of extinction. By clearing land for cities and farms, and by dumping waste chemicals into rivers and lakes, people can make habitats unfit for many living things. People have also hunted some animals to extinction.

Some of the World's Endangered Animals and Plants

Animal or Plant	Range
Florida cougar	the Everglades of Florida
whooping crane	the Texas coast (in winter)
snow leopard	the mountains of Central Asia
giant panda	western China
Arabian oryx	the Arabian Peninsula
mountain gorilla	the mountains of Central Africa
Devil's Hole pupfish	Death Valley, on the California/Nevada border
Rio Palenque mahogany	the forest of western Ecuador

Unnatural Change

Natural disasters aren't the only changes that can have deadly effects on an ecosystem. Ecosystems are in a delicate balance between the energy and nutrients that enter the system and those that leave it or are used up. Sometimes too many nutrients enter an ecosystem. Excessive minerals may be brought in by floodwaters or rain. Fertilizers may be drained from farmland. Materials that an ecosystem is unable to use up or get rid of are considered *pollution*.

Harmful chemicals may enter an ecosystem, too. For example, industrial waste from factories or pesticides from farmlands may soak into topsoil or pour into rivers, streams, or oceans and pollute the water. Fumes from automobiles and factory smokestacks may stream into the atmosphere and pollute the air that plants and animals (including humans) need to survive. Garbage from cities and towns may build up in waste areas called landfills. The effects of some kinds of pollution created by people can endanger ecosystems all over the world.

▶ OKAY FOR NOW, BUT WHAT ABOUT LATER?

Often pollution is the result of not thinking far enough ahead. When people in the Ohio Valley wished to control the air pollution from factory smokestacks in their area, they required the factories to build their smokestacks higher. It worked, and the pollution lessened in the Ohio Valley. Unfortunately, it was later learned that the pollution only went elsewhere–into the atmosphere and down as acid rain falling on New England.

Environmental Problems

acid rain: Gases spewed into the air by cars, chimneys, and smokestacks make rainwater up to 30 times more acidic than it usually is. When this rain falls, it can kill forests and poison lakes and streams.

global warming: By burning fossil fuels for energy, it is possible that people are adding too much carbon dioxide gas to the air. This could cause global air temperatures to rise. Some scientists predict that higher temperatures could cause the polar ice caps to melt, raising sea levels all over the world and changing Earth's weather patterns.

desertification: People often overuse the land where they live. Farmers may plant crops over and over again, using up all the nutrients in the soil. People may cut down all the trees for firewood and allow their cattle to eat all the grass. All that is left is a desert wasteland that cannot be used to grow crops or trees.

greenhouse effect: the trapping of heat in the atmosphere by carbon dioxide gas. The CO_2 traps heat much the way glass does in a plant greenhouse.

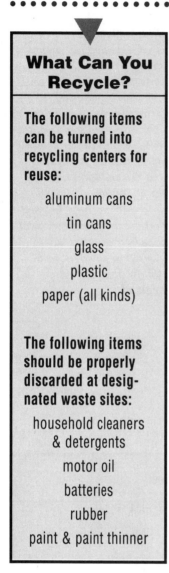

What Can You Recycle?

The following items can be turned into recycling centers for reuse:

aluminum cans

tin cans

glass

plastic

paper (all kinds)

The following items should be properly discarded at designated waste sites:

household cleaners & detergents

motor oil

batteries

rubber

paint & paint thinner

▶ CAN'T LIVE WITHOUT IT

While runaway global warming could spell disaster, the greenhouse effect in itself is not a bad thing. The carbon dioxide in the atmosphere helps to keep the air warm enough to make Earth's average overall temperature a comfy 70°F (21°C). Without the greenhouse effect, the average temperature would be about -20°F (-94°C)!

Recycling: An Earth-Friendly Approach

You can choose to do your part to protect Earth's ecosystems by conserving energy and resources, and by trying not to disturb local ecosystems. Another "Earth-friendly" choice is to *recycle*. That means to reuse materials over and over whenever possible, rather than using new materials. Recycled paper is made from old paper that has already been used. It takes 25 to 50 percent less energy to make recycled paper than brand-new paper.

Renewable Energy

By the time you have grandchildren, Earth's fossil fuels may be all used up. Fossil fuels are *nonrenewable* sources of energy. However, the energy from *renewable* sources, such as the wind, the tides, and the sun, will always be available. These energy sources have another big plus, too—using them does not contribute to acid rain or to global warming.

STARTLING STATISTIC

On average, in one year an acre of land with a forest of trees on it loses no topsoil, and only about one-half of one percent of its rainfall flows away as runoff. An acre of land that has been cleared bare, however, loses more than 140 tons of topsoil in a single year, and about 50 percent of the rainfall it receives drains away as runoff.

THE HUMAN BODY

· ·

The Magnificent Machine

What do you think is the most amazing machine in the world? A computer? A jet airplane? A submarine? Take a moment to look in the mirror and you will see the world's most amazing machine—the human body. Your body performs a great variety of "functions"—walking, seeing, hearing, making decisions, communicating, and much more. This machine also runs efficiently on a wide variety of fuels (different kinds of food). And in many situations, it can even repair itself. What other machine can do that?

Like all living things, your body is made up of cells—billions and billions of them. The cells are organized into special material called *tissue,* such as nerve tissue, bone tissue, muscle tissue, and skin tissue. Combinations of tissues make up *organs,* which are parts of the body that perform particular jobs. For example, your eyes are organs that help you see. Finally, combinations of

Your body works as well as it does because its many parts are highly organized.

The Major Systems of the Human Body

System	Main Job
skeletal	supporting the body
muscular	moving the body
respiratory	breathing, gas exchange
digestive	eating and digesting food
circulatory	moving blood and nutrients throughout the body
renal	getting rid of wastes; regulating the amount of water in the body
immune	protecting the body from disease
sensory	learning about the outside world through the senses
nervous	analyzing information from the senses; communicating instructions within the body
endocrine	sending and receiving instructions (through chemicals) within the body
reproductive	producing young

▶ **A Bounty of Bones**
More than half the bones in your body are in your hands and feet. There are 54 bones in your two hands and 52 in your two feet!

organs and other structures, such as muscles and glands, make up entire *systems.* Your circulatory system, for instance, includes all your blood vessels and blood, as well as the heart that pumps the blood throughout your body. The many systems in your body work together so you can sense the world around you, work, eat, play, and do all the other things you do each and every day. Taking care of your body is your job. For it to work properly, you must eat the right foods, keep clean, and get plenty of rest and exercise.

The science of the human body has two main branches. *Physiology* is the study of how the body works. *Anatomy* is the study of the structure of the body.

The Skeletal System

You've probably seen a picture of a jellyfish. Without your skeleton, you would look a lot like this squishy sea creature. Your skeleton is made up of over two hundred bones that provide support for your body, and give it its shape. Your bones also protect your internal organs and are anchoring points for the muscles that allow you to move.

• •

cartilage: hard but flexible tissue. Cartilage is found not only between the bones of the spine, but also in a variety of other joints and in the nose and ears.

ligaments: bands of tough, flexible material that connect bones at joints.
• •

How Do Broken Bones Heal?

Climbing trees, in-line skating, and bicycling are fun, but sometimes an accidental fall can lead to a broken bone. Fortunately, as soon as a break takes place, your body goes to work to mend it. A protective covering around bones called the *periosteum* contains special cells that can produce the new bone cells your body needs for growth and repair. When a bone is broken, a blood clot forms at the break. This is replaced by a "plug" of new bone cells called a *callus.* The callus binds the broken parts together and eventually the bone heals.

Healing of a Broken Bone

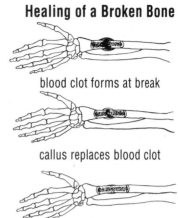

blood clot forms at break

callus replaces blood clot

bone heals

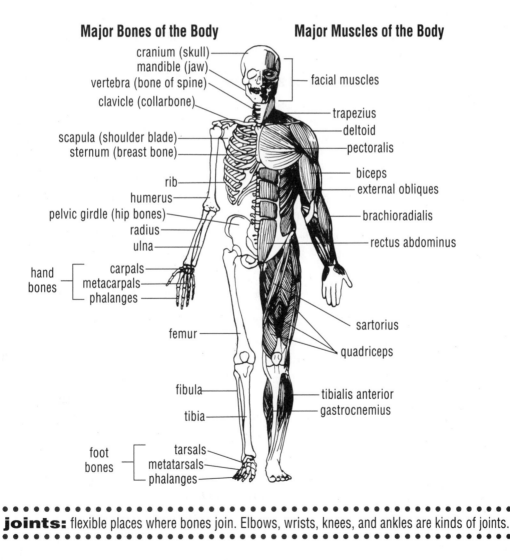

Major Bones of the Body

- cranium (skull)
- mandible (jaw)
- vertebra (bone of spine)
- clavicle (collarbone)
- scapula (shoulder blade)
- sternum (breast bone)
- rib
- humerus
- pelvic girdle (hip bones)
- radius
- ulna
- hand bones
  - carpals
  - metacarpals
  - phalanges
- femur
- fibula
- tibia
- foot bones
  - tarsals
  - metatarsals
  - phalanges

Major Muscles of the Body

- facial muscles
- trapezius
- deltoid
- pectoralis
- biceps
- external obliques
- brachioradialis
- rectus abdominus
- sartorius
- quadriceps
- tibialis anterior
- gastrocnemius

joints: flexible places where bones join. Elbows, wrists, knees, and ankles are kinds of joints.

▶ KEEPING IT TOGETHER

Skeletal muscles are attached to bones by tough bands called tendons. *When a muscle contracts, it pulls on the tendon, which pulls on the bone, causing it to move. You can easily feel the largest tendon in your body, called the Achilles tendon. It runs along the back of your ankle.*

IT'S EASIER TO BE HAPPY

It takes 43 different muscles to frown, but to smile it takes just 17!

AND NOW A WORD FROM YOUR VOCAL CORDS

Place your hand on your throat, then swallow. The lump you feel moving up and down is your larynx. Inside the larynx are two stretchy bands of tissue called the vocal cords. Air passing between the vocal cords causes them to vibrate and thus produce sounds. By "shaping" the sounds with your throat, tongue, lips, and teeth, you can form words.

The Muscular System

Muscles are the parts of the body that allow you to move, but even when you are standing perfectly still, your muscles are hard at work. They are helping you to breathe, move air, blood, and nutrients throughout your body, and maintain your balance.

Muscles are bundles of stretchy tissue that are able to contract (shorten), then relax (lengthen). Some muscles are *involuntary*, which means you do not have to think about moving them. The heart muscle and the muscles that move your food along your intestines are involuntary muscles. Other types of muscles are *voluntary*. You can make them move when you want them to. The muscles in your arms and legs are voluntary muscles.

types of muscles

skeletal muscle—voluntary muscle attached to a bone. Skeletal muscles are responsible for voluntary movement, such as running, catching a ball, petting a cat, or smiling. Some skeletal muscles can be involuntary, too, such as those that move the rib cage during breathing.

smooth muscle—involuntary muscle that lines the walls of an internal organ, such as the stomach and blood vessels. Smooth muscle controls things that work without having to think about them, such as digestion of food and circulation of blood.

cardiac muscle—involuntary muscle that controls the beating of the heart.

The Respiratory System

If you have ever tried to hold your breath during an underwater dive, you know it doesn't take long before you must surface. Like all animals, people must take in oxygen to survive. The cells of our bodies need oxygen to help convert energy into a form that the body can use. At the same time, our bodies need to get rid of carbon dioxide, which is a waste product of the cells. The process of taking in oxygen (O_2) and *eliminating* carbon dioxide (CO_2) is known as *gas exchange*, and it is handled by the respiratory system.

trachea (also called the windpipe)—air passageway from the mouth to the lungs.

larynx (also called the voice box)—structure at the top of the trachea that holds the vocal cords, which are responsible for producing sound.

bronchi (singular: bronchus)—branches of the trachea that enter the lungs.

bronchioles—small branches at the ends of the bronchi.

lungs—pair of organs in which gas exchange takes place.

alveoli (singular: alveolus)—clusters of tiny, balloonlike sacs at the ends of the bronchioles.

diaphragm—sheet of muscle below the lungs.

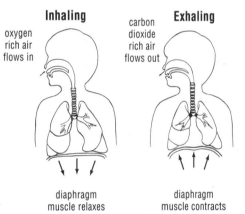

How Do You Breathe?

When you inhale, air travels through the air passages all the way to the tiny alveoli (about 3 million of them). Each alveolus is surrounded by tiny blood vessels called *capillaries*. Oxygen in the alveoli is transferred across the walls of the alveoli into the capillaries. At the same time, carbon dioxide carried by the blood is transferred out of the capillaries into the alveoli. Then the carbon dioxide is pushed out of your lungs and you *exhale*.

Inhaling

oxygen rich air flows in

diaphragm muscle relaxes

Exhaling

carbon dioxide rich air flows out

diaphragm muscle contracts

The movements of the diaphragm and rib muscles cause your chest cavity to expand and contract, drawing in and pushing out air.

The Digestive System

Food is the fuel that provides the energy to keep your body going. But the food must be broken down before the body's cells can use the nutrients in it. That is the job of the digestive system.

The food you eat goes through a long tube called the *alimentary canal*. During this journey, the food is broken down by digestive juices into simpler forms. Eventually, the nutrients in the food are absorbed into the blood and carried to all the cells of the body. At the same time, the unusable parts of food are eliminated.

▶ OUT OF CONTROL

Sometimes the diaphragm muscle contracts uncontrollably and repeatedly. When that happens, the lungs draw in short, sharp breaths of air—hiccups! The vocal cords slamming shut make the funny "hic" sound. No one knows what causes hiccups to start, but some cases have reportedly lasted for years!

mouth—opening where food enters the body and digestion begins.

esophagus—large tube that leads from the mouth to the stomach.

stomach—stretchy, baglike organ where digestion continues. Most of the harmful bacteria in food are killed by acids in the stomach.

small intestine—coiled tube in which most digestion takes place. The walls of the small intestine absorb the nutrients and water in food, which then enter the bloodstream and travel to all parts of the body.

large intestine—another tube, larger than the small intestine. Waste material from the small intestine passes into the large intestine. The main job of the large intestine is to absorb water from this material.

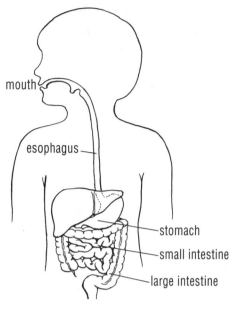

The Circulatory System

Nutrients from food and oxygen from air must reach the body cells that need them. Your circulatory system is like a delivery service. It includes the *heart* and *blood*, as well as the network of tubes, called *blood vessels*, that carry blood throughout your body. Blood delivers nutrients and oxygen to all of the body's cells. It also carries carbon dioxide and waste products away from the cells.

The Heart

The heart is a remarkable organ that pumps blood throughout the entire body. It pumps continuously at an average of about once every second, and it will continue to do that as long as you live. Each beat of your heart sends blood pulsing through your body. The number of pulses per minute is called your heart rate. When a male adult is resting, his average heart rate is about 70 beats per minute. The resting rate of a 10-year-old child is higher than that. To find out what your *heart rate* is, place two fingertips on your neck just below your jaw on either side of your vocal cords.

You should be able to feel your pulse. Watching the second hand of a clock, count the number of beats you feel in 15 seconds, then multiply that number by four. The result is your resting heart rate. If you check your heart rate again after you have been exercising, will it be higher or lower?

The Circulatory System

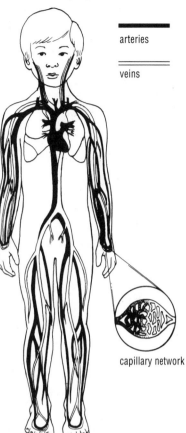

arteries

veins

capillary network

The Body's Blood Vessels

arteries: vessels that carry blood away from the heart to other parts of the body.

veins: vessels that carry blood from other parts of the body to the heart. Special valves in some veins, such as those in the legs, prevent blood from flowing back in the wrong direction.

capillaries: very thin vessels that join arteries with veins.

▶ THAT'S QUITE A STRETCH

Blood vessels reach every part of your body. If your blood vessels were stretched out end to end, they would circle the globe nearly three times!

parts of the heart

atria (singular: atrium)—the two upper chambers of the heart.

ventricles—the two lower chambers of the heart.

aorta—artery that carries oxygen-rich blood out of the heart to the rest of the body. The aorta is the largest artery in the body.

pulmonary arteries—two arteries that carry oxygen-poor (and carbon-dioxide-rich) blood to the lungs.

superior vena cava—vein that brings oxygen-poor blood from the upper body to the heart.

inferior vena cava—vein that brings oxygen-poor blood from the lower body to the heart.

pulmonary veins—four veins that carry oxygen-rich blood from the lungs to the heart.

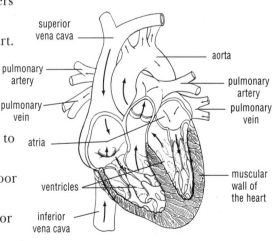

superior vena cava

aorta

pulmonary artery

pulmonary artery

pulmonary vein

pulmonary vein

atria

muscular wall of the heart

ventricles

inferior vena cava

The arrows show the direction of blood flow. Valves prevent blood from flowing backward.

The Sensory System

The Senses	
Organ	**Sense**
eyes	sight
nose	smell
ear	hearing
tongue	taste
skin	touch

The organs of your sensory system are your windows on the world. Think back to the last time you were playing outside. What was it like? Could you see and hear other children playing? Could you smell the grass and feel the warmth of the sun on your skin? These questions may seem simple, but without your sensory organs, you wouldn't know the answers to any of them. Your sensory organs gather information about your surroundings, then send the information to the brain along nerve pathways. The brain then interprets the information it receives.

Sight

We live in a world of light that is produced either by luminous objects or reflected from nonluminous objects (see page 13). When light enters your eye, it travels to a special lining at the back called the *retina*. There, nerves are stimulated and send messages to the brain. The brain then interprets the messages and you are able to see.

parts of the eye

sclera—tough, outer covering (the "white") of the eye.
cornea—transparent area of the sclera.
iris—colored part of the eye. Muscles in the iris contract and relax to change the size of the pupil.
pupil—opening at the center of the iris that lets in light.
lens—clear structure behind the iris that focuses light rays.
retina—inner layer of tissue at the back of the eye. The retina contains light-sensitive cells called *rods* and *cones*. The rods see only black and white, but work very well in dim light, while the cones see color.
optic nerve—nerve pathway that carries information from the eye to the brain.

sclera
lens
iris
retina
pupil
optic nerve
cornea
iris

Sound

Sound is actually just waves of vibrations in the air. When these vibrations reach your ear, they travel through the ear canal to inside your ear. The vibrations stimulate nerves, which then send messages to the brain. The brain interprets the messages as sound and you are able to hear.

•••••••••••••••••••••▶ parts of the ear

pinna—flap of skin and cartilage at the outer edge of the ear canal. The pinna helps to direct sound into the ear canal.

ear canal—short channel leading to the middle ear.

eardrum—thin layer of tissue at the end of the ear canal. The eardrum vibrates when sound waves strike it.

malleus, incus, and stapes—three bones of the middle ear. These tiny bones transmit vibrations from the eardrum to the oval window.

oval window—tissue-covered opening between the middle ear and inner ear.

semicircular canals—three looped tubes that help to control the body's sense of balance.

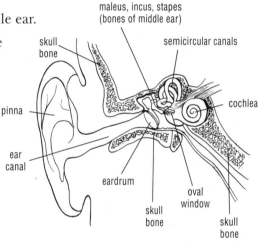

cochlea—coiled, fluid-filled organ lined with tiny hairlike cells. Sound waves cause these cells to move, stimulating nerves that carry sound information to the brain.

Taste

Chemicals in food are responsible for taste. When food is dissolved by saliva in the mouth, these chemicals come in contact with special cells called taste buds that are mainly on the tongue. These buds send information to the brain. The brain can interpret four different tastes: sweet, sour, bitter, and salty.

Taste Centers on the Tongue

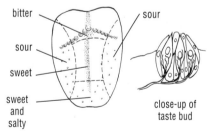

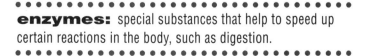

enzymes: special substances that help to speed up certain reactions in the body, such as digestion.

Smell

Odors are actually caused by tiny chemical particles in the air. When you breathe, you draw in some of these particles. The particles then come in contact with cells in the nasal passages called *olfactory rods*. When that happens, the rods send signals to the *olfactory bulbs* and then to the brain, which it interprets as smells.

Touch

The sense of touch includes sensations of pressure, pain, heat, and cold. When nerve endings, mostly in the skin, are stimulated by any of these sensations, they send messages to the brain. The brain interprets the messages and sends instructions to various parts of your body so actions can be taken, such as putting on a sweater when you're cold.

The Nervous System

Once your senses pick up information from the outside world (such as "a speeding baseball is heading straight toward me"), that information must somehow reach the brain. Then the brain has to interpret the information and decide what your next move should be (such as "swing the bat with your arms and slam that baseball into orbit"). Those instructions then must be sent to all of the organs and muscles involved in carrying out the action. The system that handles the interpretation of the outside environment, as well as the internal communication going on in your body, is the nervous system.

The nervous system controls all actions of the body, both voluntary and involuntary. There are two parts to the nervous system. The *central nervous system* is made up of the brain and the spinal cord. The *peripheral nervous system* is made up of all the nerves of the body outside of the central nervous system.

▶ THE NOSE KNOWS
People can recognize as many as 3,000 different odors.

the immune system

You might be amazed to know there is a battle going on right in your own body. Throughout your life, you are regularly exposed to tiny organisms called *viruses* and *bacteria* (also known as germs) that can make you sick. Your skin helps to keep out some germs, but others may get into your body through your mouth, nose, or cuts in your skin. Then your main line of defense is your immune system.

Part of the immune system—white blood cells called *lymphocytes*—produce disease-fighting *antibodies* that can destroy germs.

▶ HIGH-SPEED TRAVELERS
Nerve impulses travel to the brain as fast as 250 miles (402.5 km) per hour!

Partners

Think back to the last time you had a cold and your nose was stuffy. It was probably difficult to taste food. That's because the senses of smell and taste work together as partners. Here is a way that you and your own partner can test this for yourselves.

You Will Need:
▲ blindfold ▲ lemon juice ▲ vinegar ▲ salt ▲ sugar ▲ chopped apple ▲ chopped potato ▲ six teaspoons

1. Place a small amount of each of the foods listed above in a separate teaspoon.

2. Cover your eyes with the blindfold and pinch your nose closed.

3. Ask your friend to help you taste the lemon and the vinegar, one at a time, without telling you which is which. Is it hard to tell the difference between the two? Now try it without holding your nose. Is it easier to tell?

4. Repeat the test using salt and sugar, then apple and potato.

What conclusions can you draw from your experiments?

Neurons

The entire nervous system includes about 100 billion cells called *neurons.* The neurons carry electrical and chemical messages, or *nerve impulses,* throughout the body. *Sensory neurons* transport signals from the sense organs to the central nervous system. *Motor neurons* carry signals from the central nervous system to the muscles and internal organs. At this very moment, about 3 million nerve impulses are racing through your body.

Neurons have a *cell body,* a long "tail" called the *axon,* and branches at either end that communicate either with other nerves or with parts of the body such as sense organs or muscles. There is a space between the neurons called a *synapse.* A neuron sends chemical *messengers* across the synapse to chemical receptors on the next neuron.

neuron

cell body

synapse

axon

Certain messengers "fit" certain receptors much the way a key fits a lock.

neuron

WOULD YOU BELIEVE?

The longest neurons in the body are those that run from the base of the spine to the big toes of each foot. Their actual length depends on how tall you are.

nerve: a bundle of neurons, blood vessels, and supportive tissue. There are usually both sensory and motor neurons in a single nerve.

spinal cord: the large bundle of nerves that runs through the tubelike opening in your spine.

Central Nervous System

The main control center of your body is your brain. You might think of your brain as being your body's "central government." Different parts of the brain control different things.

parts of the brain

cerebrum—the part of the brain that controls voluntary movement, speech, the senses and perception, decision making, learning, memory, thought and reasoning.

cerebellum—the part of the brain that coordinates muscle movement and governs balance.

brain stem—the part of the brain that controls automatic functions, such as breathing and heartbeat.

thalamus—brain part that relays much of the incoming sensory information from the body to the cerebrum.

hypothalamus—control center for automatic functions, such as breathing, digestion, and blood circulation.

pituitary gland—"master gland" that controls other glands and many body processes, such as growth and water balance. The pituitary is controlled by the hypothalamus.

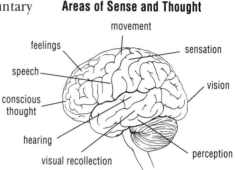

Areas of Sense and Thought

movement
feelings
speech
sensation
conscious thought
vision
hearing
visual recollection
perception

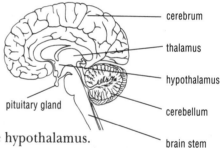

Cross Section of the Brain

cerebrum
thalamus
hypothalamus
pituitary gland
cerebellum
brain stem

the endocrine system

Your nervous system is the high-speed messenger system of your body. But there is another messenger system, too—the endocrine system. It sends slower, chemical messages by way of the blood. The messengers are called *hormones* and they are produced by special structures called *endocrine glands*. Listed below are some major endocrine glands and hormones:

Gland	Hormone	Function
hypothalamus	releasing factors	signals the pituitary gland
pituitary	growth hormone	controls growth of the body
thyroid	thyroxine	controls heat and energy production
pancreas	insulin and glucagon	controls levels of sugar in the blood
adrenal	adrenaline	controls emergency reactions such as causing your heart to beat faster

the renal system

Would you believe that about two-thirds of your body is made up of water? And each time you eat and drink, you take in more water. Although you lose some of this water when you exhale and when you perspire, if it weren't for your renal system you would swell up like a sponge! The two kidneys are the main organs of the renal system. Besides controlling how much water there is in the body, the kidneys are also responsible for filtering out waste materials, such as salt and a waste product called urea, from the blood.

The Reproductive System

One of the characteristics of living things is that they are able to reproduce themselves. People reproduce by *sexual reproduction.* In other words, a male and female join to produce a new human being that has traits from both of his or her parents.

▶ parts of the female reproductive system

ovaries—pair of organs in which female sex cells, or ova (eggs), are produced. A single egg is called an ovum.

fallopian tubes (also called uterine tubes)—thin tubes that carry eggs to the uterus. Fertilization (when two sex cells, one from the mother and one from the father, combine) takes place in the fallopian tubes.

uterus—hollow organ in which a fertilized egg develops.

vagina—canal through which sperm enter the female body.

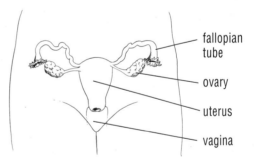

▶ parts of the male reproductive system

testes—pair of organs in which male sex cells, or sperm, are produced.

scrotum—fleshy sac that contains the testes.

sperm duct—thin tube that delivers sperm from the testes to the penis.

penis—organ through which sperm are released.

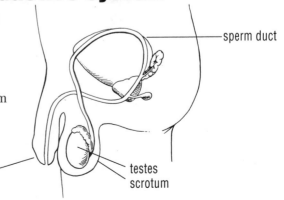

109

Teaming Up

Within the nucleus of most human cells there are 46 tiny units called chromosomes. *They are made up of strings of material called* DNA. *These strings are simply a set of instructions telling the cell what to do. Sperm and ova contain only 23 chromosomes each. When sperm and ova combine, they form a* zygote—*the first cell of a new human. The* zygote *then contains 46 chromosomes, arranged in 23 pairs, half from one parent, half from the other.*

• •

gene: a segment of a DNA molecule in a cell. There are up to 1000 genes in each molecule. These genes, some from each parent, determine such things as how tall a person may be, what color eyes he or she will have, or if the person may develop a certain disease.

• •

A New Baby

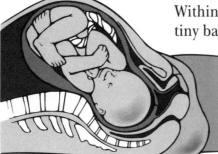

The development of a new baby begins when fertilization occurs. The zygote divides into two cells, which then divide into four cells, and so on. Within a week of fertilization, the new baby is a tiny ball of at least 64 cells called an *embryo*. The embryo is attached to the wall of the mother's uterus. The baby continues to grow and develop. After about 40 weeks from fertilization, the baby turns head down and travels from its mother's uterus to the outside world to be born.

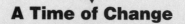

A Time of Change

Changes take place in your body as you develop from a child to an adult. The first stage of this development is called puberty. Girls usually begin puberty at about age 11. For boys, this stage often begins at about 13. Here are some of the changes that take place at puberty:

Boys	Girls
grow taller	grow taller
underarm and pubic hair develop	underarm and pubic hair develop
facial hair grows	breasts develop
voice becomes deeper	hips widen

10 SPACE

The Solar System and Beyond

Have you ever looked into the night sky and wished you could walk on the moon or visit a distant star? In a way you can with the help of some amazing tools. Optical and radio telescopes "see" into the distant reaches of our universe. Space probes take full-color pictures, and even broadcast television images that let us "journey" into space.

radio telescope

Astronomy is the study of the universe and all of the stars, planets, moons, and other objects in it. These objects number in the trillions and trillions. The first question you might ask is, where did all these celestial objects come from? According to one theory, about 15 billion years ago, everything in the universe was squeezed into a tiny speck much smaller than a grain of sand. Then, suddenly, something caused the speck to explode outward. This explosion is known as the *Big Bang*.

Spiral galaxy NGC 2997

Over the many millions of years that followed, stars and galaxies began to form. After at least 7½ billion years, our own solar system began to take shape. Fortunately, the planet Earth formed at just the right distance from the sun so that life was able to develop and survive here. But is Earth the only planet of its kind in the universe? What are the other planets in our solar system like? Will the sun shine forever? How long will the universe last? These are some of the questions that astronomers hope to answer by exploring our solar system and the things that lie beyond it.

universe: all the matter and energy that exists anywhere and everywhere. In other words, the universe is everything we know of.

Incredible Distances

The distances between objects in space are so great that astronomers do not work with ordinary units of measurement like miles and kilometers. Instead, they work with the following units of measure.

astronomical unit (AU): average distance between the sun and Earth, or about 93 million miles (149,600,000 km). It would take a person driving a car at 55 miles (89 km) per hour about 190 years to travel one AU.

light-year: about 6 trillion miles (9.5 trillion km), or the distance light travels through space in one Earth year. The same person driving a car at 55 miles (89 km) per hour would take more than *12 million years* to travel one light-year.

parsec: distance equaling about 3¼ light-years. The person driving a car at 55 miles (89 km) per hour would take nearly *40 million years* to travel one parsec!

The Solar System

The *solar system* is made up of our local star, the Sun, and all of the planets, moons, asteroids, and other objects that circle it. The outermost region of the solar system is thought to be an area occupied by what is known as the Oort Cloud. This is where many astronomers think comets come from (see page 118).

Relative Sizes of the Planets

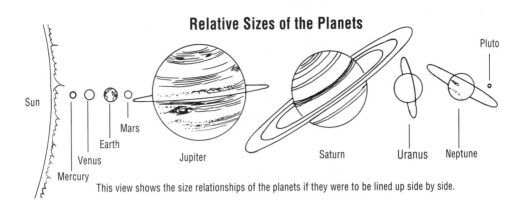

This view shows the size relationships of the planets if they were to be lined up side by side.

Relative Distances of the Planets

Close-Up of Inner Planets

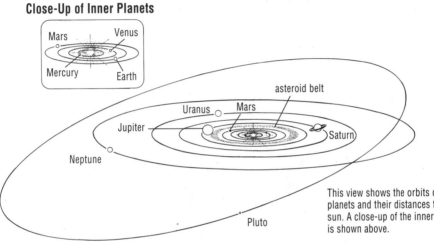

This view shows the orbits of the planets and their distances from the sun. A close-up of the inner planets is shown above.

The View from Earth

Imagine you are riding in a car. As you pass things along the road, such as trees, they seem to be moving in the opposite direction from you, but you know it is really the car that is moving. If you were to take a journey in space, to you it may look like the sun makes a daily trip across the sky from east to west. At night, the planets and stars seem to travel across the sky, too. But it is the Earth that is moving. It is turning, or *rotating*, from west to east. It takes 24 hours to make one rotation.

The Earth also completes one journey, or orbit,

The Scientists

Nicolaus Copernicus
(Poland, 1473–1543)

Copernicus was a Polish astronomer. During his time, people believed Earth stood still in space and everything else in the universe revolved around it. He believed the Earth actually rotated on its axis and that the planets revolved around the sun.

axis: imaginary line that runs through the center of the Earth from the North Pole to the South Pole.

ecliptic: apparent path the sun and planets take across the sky.

113

Earth's Orbit and the Seasons

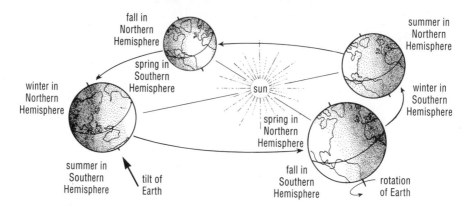

around the sun in about 365 days, or one *year*. As the planet moves along, your view of space changes. That is why you see different star groups, or *constellations*, at different times of the year. This journey is also what causes the four seasons: spring, summer, fall, and winter. The Earth is tilted on its *axis*, and at different points along its path, one of its halves, or hemispheres, is pointed toward the sun. The hemisphere tilted toward the sun experiences summer and the hemisphere tilted away shivers through winter. The points in between are spring and fall.

What Are Constellations?

Constellations are groups of stars related to each other by how they appear to an observer on Earth, such as you. Have you ever completed a dot-to-dot puzzle, making a picture by connecting the dots? Constellations are like huge dot-to-dot puzzles in the night sky.

Several thousand years ago, ancient stargazers saw these star groups as rough outlines of animals and people.

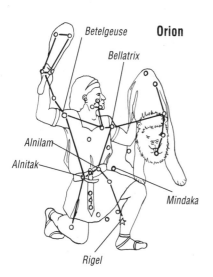

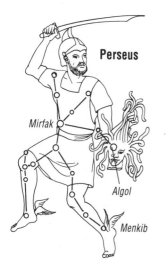

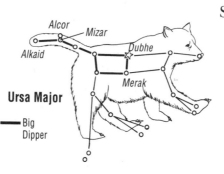

114

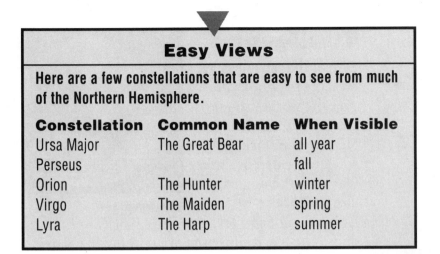

Easy Views

Here are a few constellations that are easy to see from much of the Northern Hemisphere.

Constellation	Common Name	When Visible
Ursa Major	The Great Bear	all year
Perseus		fall
Orion	The Hunter	winter
Virgo	The Maiden	spring
Lyra	The Harp	summer

The Sun

Quick, what is the nearest star to Earth? If you answered the sun, you are right. The sun is a star and it is the center of our solar system. The sun is not a particularly large star, but it takes up as much space as 1 million planets the size of Earth.

The incredible heat and pressure at the sun's core causes atoms of hydrogen to join together to form helium. This is called *nuclear fusion.* As a result of the fusion process, energy is given off. The energy radiates into space, and some of it reaches Earth as heat and light.

The sun with a dramatic prominence (photo taken with an ultraviolet spectro-heliograph camera)

▶ SAFETY FIRST
NEVER LOOK DIRECTLY AT THE SUN WITH THE NAKED EYE OR PARTICULARLY THROUGH A TELESCOPE OR BINOCULARS. THIS COULD CAUSE SEVERE EYE DAMAGE. If you wish to observe the sun, your local planetarium probably has telescopes set up with special filters for solar viewing.

Sun Facts

average distance from Earth:	93 million miles (149,600,000 km)
diameter at the poles:	864,000 miles (1,391,000 km)
age:	4.5 billion years
rotation at the equator:	25 Earth days
surface temperature:	10,000°F (5540°C)

HANDS ON!

Measuring the Moon

Sometimes, when it's close to the horizon, the moon appears larger than when it is high in the sky. Is it really larger, or is it just an optical illusion? Try this experiment and find out.

You Will Need:
▲ flat piece of glass (as from a picture frame)
▲ pair of work gloves
▲ crayon or marker

1. Wear work gloves when handling the glass. As the moon appears over the horizon, look at it through the square of glass held out at arm's length and trace its shape onto the glass with a crayon.

2. After the moon is high in the sky, look at it again through the glass. Does it still fill the circle you drew earlier? What conclusions can you draw from this observation?

The Moon

One of the most familiar faces to people all over the world just may be the "Man in the Moon." The "face" is actually formed by dark plains on the lunar surface called seas, or, in Latin, *maria* (*mare* for just

The full moon

one). The maria, however, are nothing like seas on Earth. They formed billions of years ago as molten rock flowed through cracks in the moon's surface and hardened. Also, more than 300,000 meteorite craters dot the side of the moon that faces the Earth, and there are even more on the other side.

the phases of the moon ◀·······················

You're probably familiar with the changing appearance of the moon each month. These changes are called the *phases* of the moon. Half of the moon's surface is always lit by the sun, but over a little less than 30 days, you see changing amounts of that sunlit area as the moon moves in orbit around Earth.

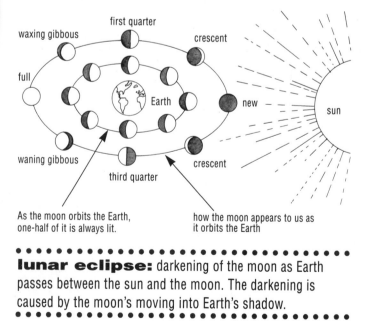

first quarter
waxing gibbous
crescent
full
Earth
new
sun
waning gibbous
third quarter
crescent

As the moon orbits the Earth, one-half of it is always lit.

how the moon appears to us as it orbits the Earth

•••••••••••••••••••••••••••••••••
lunar eclipse: darkening of the moon as Earth passes between the sun and the moon. The darkening is caused by the moon's moving into Earth's shadow.
•••••••••••••••••••••••••••••••••

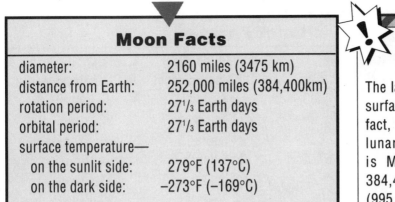

Moon Facts	
diameter:	2160 miles (3475 km)
distance from Earth:	252,000 miles (384,400km)
rotation period:	27⅓ Earth days
orbital period:	27⅓ Earth days
surface temperature—	
on the sunlit side:	279°F (137°C)
on the dark side:	−273°F (−169°C)

RECORD SETTERS

The largest mare on the surface of the moon (in fact, the largest of any lunar surface feature) is Mare Imbrium at 384,400 square miles (995,595 sq km).

The Planets

The nine known planets in the solar system are Mercury, Venus, Earth, Mars, Jupiter, Saturn, Uranus, Neptune, and Pluto.

The four inner planets (Mercury, Venus, Earth, and Mars) all have rocky surfaces. The four outer planets (Jupiter, Saturn, Uranus, and Neptune) are giant gas planets. Tiny Pluto is usually the outermost planet of all. It probably has a rocky core, but its surface is a thick layer of ice. Pluto has not yet been visited by a space probe, so we can't be certain what its surface is like.

▶ TRADING PLACES

The orbit of Pluto is tilted compared to that of the other planets. It is also very long and oval in shape. Normally, Pluto is the outermost planet, but because of its unusual orbit, Pluto trades places with Neptune for 20 years at a time. It is at this point now and will not return to its usual rank until 1999.

Earth

Jupiter

Saturn

Uranus

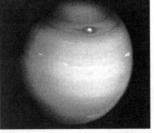

Neptune

▶ RINGS AND THINGS

Our planetary neighborhood contains more than 60 moons, most of which circle the giant gas planets. These planets are also circled by rings made of rock and ice. The rings of Saturn are the most spectacular. They have a total diameter of about 200,000 miles (322,000 km) across!

Planet Facts

Planet	Diameter (in miles)	(in km)	Length of Day (in Earth hours/days)	Length of Year (in Earth days/years)
Mercury	3030	4880	58.6 days	87.9 days
Venus	7520	12,109	243 days	224 days
Earth	7970	12,835	24 hours	365.2 days
Mars	4210	6780	24.6 hours	687 days
Jupiter	88,650	142,725	9.8 hours	11.6 years
Saturn	74,565	120,050	10.2 hours	29.4 years
Uranus	32,115	51,705	17.3 hours	84 years
Neptune	30,760	49,520	15.8 hours	165 years
Pluto	1375	2215	6.3 days	247.8 years

Other Members of the Solar System

Asteroids

Asteroid means "starlike," but you are not likely to confuse these chunks of metal and rock with stars. Most of the asteroids in the solar system circle around the sun in a wide band between Mars and Jupiter, called the *asteroid belt* (see art on page 113). For the most part, they are small. In fact, only seven asteroids have a diameter greater than 200 miles (320 km).

Comets

If you are very lucky, you may someday see a comet as it makes its way in orbit around the sun. As a ball of frozen gas and dust, a comet is very much like a rather large dirty snowball. As it nears the sun, it develops a shining halo of gas called a *coma*. A comet may also develop a pair of long, glowing tails: a curved dust tail and a long, straight tail of gas.

Halley's Comet

optical telescope: instrument for viewing distant objects with the eye. A telescope makes objects appear larger, closer, and brighter. There are two basic types of optical telescopes—the reflecting and the refracting—but if you took them apart you would find they are made of some of the same parts.

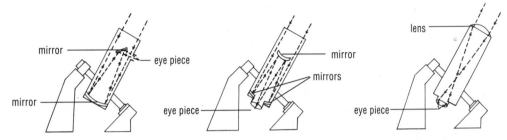

Newtonian reflecting telescope   **Cassegrainian reflecting telescope**   **refracting telescope**

objective lens: light from the object being viewed enters the telescope through the objective lens. This is the main element of a refracting telescope.

eyepiece: small lens that enlarges the image.

primary mirror: curved mirror that reflects light. This is the main element of a reflecting telescope.

secondary mirror: mirror that reflects light to the eyepiece.

Meteoroids

When you look at pictures of the rocky planets and moons of the solar system, you might notice that most have something in common. Their surfaces are often covered with craters of all different sizes. Craters are usually the result of collisions with meteoroids. Earth's craters are often worn away by erosion, but there is plenty of evidence that our planet has not been spared.

A *meteoroid* is a chunk or a grain of rock traveling through space. When it enters Earth's atmosphere, a meteoroid is probably moving at about 45,000 miles (72,000 km) per hour. As it plunges earthward, it usually heats up and disintegrates, leaving behind a glowing streak of light known as a meteor (or "shooting star").

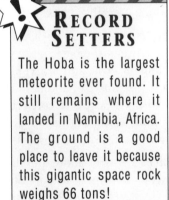

RECORD SETTERS

The Hoba is the largest meteorite ever found. It still remains where it landed in Namibia, Africa. The ground is a good place to leave it because this gigantic space rock weighs 66 tons!

▶ **WHAT'S A METEORITE?**

Thousands of meteoroids enter our atmosphere every year. Most weigh less than an ounce and burn up completely. Some actually crash into the ground. When they do, they are called meteorites.

Beyond the Solar System

The Stars

How good do you think your eyesight is? Can you see something that is a mile away. Ten miles? How about a hundred miles? Did you answer "no"? Well, you can! When you look up at the stars, you are looking at objects that are *trillions* of miles away!

Some stars are small and dim, others are huge and bright, but they all have some things in common. They are balls of incredibly hot gas. During their lifetimes, stars all produce energy through the process of nuclear fusion.

the life cycle of a star

An average-sized star, such as our sun, has a life span of about 10 billion years. This chart shows the stages that occur from the "birth" to "death" of the average star.

stage 1—A star begins its life as a huge spinning cloud of gas and dust. At this stage, it is known as a *protostar*, which literally means "before a star."

stage 2—Over about 10 million years, the tremendous pressure at the core of the gas and dust cloud causes the cloud to grow hotter and hotter. When the core reaches a temperature of about 25,000,000°F (13,800,000°C), hydrogen begins to convert to helium in a reaction known as nuclear fusion. In other words, the cloud ignites, and the protostar is now a star.

stage 3—After about 10 billion years, the star uses up the hydrogen fuel in its core and begins to die. First, it expands into a *red giant star*. (When our own sun expands to become a red giant star, it will envelop and destroy the planets of Mercury and Venus.)

stage 4—Finally, the star puffs off its outer layers of gas and shrinks down.

stage 5—The star is now a *white dwarf star*—a superdense, planet-sized star that, over many more millions of years, fades to a burned-out cinder.

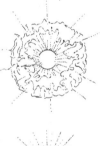

stage 1
birth

stage 2
normal life

stage 3
expansion

stage 4
puffing off
outer layer

stage 5
white dwarf

You Can't Believe Your Eyes

The way the stars look from Earth is not always the way they really are. Some stars may appear to be much brighter than other stars, but are actually smaller and dimmer. These stars only *seem* to be brighter because they are closer to us than the dimmer-looking stars. The brightness of a star is called its *magnitude.* On a scale of one to six, the brightest stars have a magnitude of one. The dimmest stars that can still be seen with the naked eye have a magnitude of six. So, the lower the number, the brighter the star. Some stars are so bright they even have minus numbers! Do you think a star with a magnitude of eight would be bright or dim?

RECORD SETTERS

Some stars, known as *red dwarfs*, are very small, cool, and dim. The dimmest star visible from Earth (with a very powerful telescope) is LHS 2924, which has an apparent magnitude of 19. If this star were to replace our sun, days on Earth would be no brighter than nights with a full moon.

a spectacular end

Stars that are much bigger and hotter than the average star are called *blue-white giants.* These stars often end their relatively short lives in the spectacular explosion we call a *supernova.*

stage 1—A hot, blue-white giant may form from a cloud of gas and dust in as little as 1 million years.

stage 2—After becoming a star, the blue-white giant burns up the supply of hydrogen at its core in as little as 10 million years. But fusion continues and, over time, new elements such as carbon are produced. A few days before the star reaches the end of its life, the core climbs to 3,000,000,000°F (1,700,000,000°C) and iron is produced. With iron at the core, fusion can't continue.

stage 3—The star begins to collapse under the force of gravity, and core temperatures soar to more than 8,000,000,000°F (4,400,000,000°C). Then the star explodes into space in a tremendous blast—a supernova.

stage 4—The supernova may leave behind a tiny, dense star called a *neutron star.* It may also continue to collapse to form what is known as a *black hole.* The gravitational attraction of a black hole is so strong that even light is unable to escape from it.

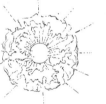

stage 1
birth

stage 2
normal life

stage 3
super nova

stage 4
neutron star
or black hole

apparent magnitude: measure of how bright a star appears to us on Earth. The apparently brightest stars are often fairly close.

absolute magnitude: measure of how bright a star would be if it were a set distance (10 parsecs) from Earth.

Galaxies

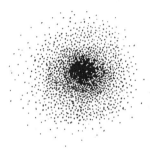

elliptical galaxy

A *galaxy* is a huge group of stars bound together by their gravitational effect on each other. Our galaxy, the Milky Way, is about 100,000 light-years across. There are at least a billion galaxies in the universe. Most are classified into several different groups by their shapes.

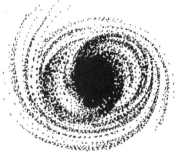

spiral galaxy

barred spiral galaxy

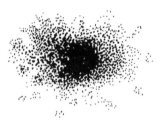

irregular galaxy

▶ EARTH'S EYES AND EARS

All around the Earth there are special places called observatories that give scientists a "glimpse" of space beyond our planet. Observatories are our "eyes" and "ears" in that they let us see and hear stars, galaxies, and more! Some of these observatories are equipped with optical telescopes and others with radio telescopes.

RECORD SETTERS

▲ The optical telescope with the largest mirror is the Keck telescope in Hawaii. The mirror is 33 feet (10 m) across.

▲ The world's largest radio telescope, located in Puerto Rico, is 1000 feet (310 km) across.

radio telescope: telescope with a receiver and an antenna designed for receiving radio waves from space. Many objects and events in space, such as pulsars, quasars, and supernovas, produce radio waves. Within our solar system, the sun and the planet Jupiter produce radio waves.

Humans in Space

On April 12, 1961, a very brave Russian cosmonaut named Yuri Gargarin climbed into a tiny capsule called *Vostok 1*. The capsule was perched atop a huge rocket. Suddenly, the rocket roared to life and carried the capsule and its passenger into both space and history. Yuri Gargarin was the first human launched into space. Since that time, courageous men and women have faced the unknown, and remarkable unmanned spacecraft and probes have journeyed to the very edge of the solar system to explore what lies beyond Earth's atmosphere.

Astronaut Edwin Aldrin, Jr., walking on the surface of the moon

First Human Steps into Space

Although it may be a long time before people visit even the nearest stars, humankind has already made the first steps on the journey.

Date	Accomplishment	Astronaut(s)	Country	Craft
4/12/61	first manned space flight	Yuri Gargarin	USSR	*Vostok 1*
2/20/62	first American in orbit	John Glenn	USA	*Friendship 7*
6/16/63	first woman in space	Valentina Tereshkova	USSR	*Vostok 6*
3/16/66	first docking in space	Neil Armstrong David Scott	USA	*Gemini 8*
10/21/69	first to travel to moon and back	Frank Borman James Lovell William Anders	USA	*Apollo 10*
7/20/69	first moon landing	Neil Armstrong Buzz Aldrin Michael Collins	USA	*Apollo 11*
4/12/81	first shuttle mission	John W. Young Robert L. Crippen	USA	*STS-1 Columbia*

USEFUL MEASUREMENTS

The sciences can be broken into many major branches, but they all have certain things in common. For one, scientists use certain units when counting and measuring. In the United States, imperial units are sometimes used, such as pounds and ounces for weight, feet and miles for length, and pints and gallons for measuring volume. The system used by most scientists, however, is the metric system. The following chart will help you to convert measurements from one system to the other.

Measurement Abbreviations

Metric	
centimeters	cm
kilometers	km
square meters	m^2
square kilometers	km^2
liters	1
grams	g
kilograms	kg

Imperial	
inches	in
feet	ft
miles	mi
square feet	ft^2
square miles	mi^2
pints	pt
gallons	gal
ounces	oz
pounds	lb

Measurement Conversions

Metric

To change metric	to imperial	multiply by
centimeters	inches	0.39
meters	feet	3.28
kilometers	miles	0.62
square meters	square feet	10.76
square kilometers	square miles	0.39
liters	pints	2.11
liters	gallons	0.26
grams	ounces	0.04
kilograms	pounds	2.21

Imperial

To change imperial	to metric	multiply by
inches	centimeters	2.54
feet	meters	0.31
miles	kilometers	1.61
square feet	square meters	0.09
square miles	square kilometers	2.59
pints	liters	0.47
gallons	liters	3.7
ounces	grams	28.35
pounds	kilograms	0.45

Temperature Conversions

Two ways used to measure temperature are by degrees Celsius (°C) and degrees Fahrenheit (°F).

Celsius to Fahrenheit:
Multiply the temperature by 9, divide the answer by 5, then add 32.
Example: 25°C x 9 ÷ 5 + 32 = 77°F

Fahrenheit to Celsius:
Subtract 32 from the temperature, multiply the answer by 5, then divide by 9.
Example: 86°F − 32 x 5 ÷ 9 = 30°C

SCIENTIFIC NAMES

Biology is the study of living things, or organisms. So that scientists all over the world, no matter what language they speak, can identify them, all living things are given two Latin names, a genus name and a species name. For example, your dog may be Rover or Spot to you, but to a biologist he is *Canis familiaris*.

Biologists organize, or classify, the living things they study into groups that share certain characteristics. The largest groups are called Kingdoms. Within each group there are smaller groups. The smaller the group, the more characteristics the organisms within it have in common with each other. The groups are:

Plants	Animals
Kingdom	Kingdom
Division	Phylum
Class	Class
Order	Order
Family	Family
Genus	Genus
Species	Species

INDEX